EDITING YEATS'S POEMS

The publication history of Yeats's poems and his own habits of composition and revision have led to particularly complex textual problems, but in his new edition of Yeats's poems Professor Finneran has been concerned to present the text as Yeats intended it to stand. Through a careful study of the surviving manuscript materials, letters and annotated copies, Professor Finneran has been able to identify the numerous changes which were introduced into the poems, after Yeats's death, by his wife and Thomas Mark, his editor at Macmillan.

Here, in describing the problems he encountered, Professor Finneran shows clearly that the various editions published to date have been unsatisfactory. He points to the significance of some of the changes in the poems to their interpretation; he discusses the question of whether, as has been suggested, Yeats was the author of some poems published under the initial 'Y' in *Hibernia* in 1882–3; and he identifies the sources for many of the songs in Yeats's plays. While explaining the reasons for reaching many of the editorial decisions he made, Professor Finneran concludes that the editing of Yeats's poems will always remain as much an art as a science.

This book is not only an essential companion to *The Poems of W. B. Yeats, A New Edition*; in tracing the history of the various editions of Yeats's poems, it also stands in its own right as a fascinating piece of literary history.

Richard J. Finneran is Professor of English at Newcomb College, Tulane University. He has previously held teaching posts at the University of Florida and New York University and has been a lecturer at the Yeats International Summer School in Sligo. Professor Finneran is well known for his work on Anglo-Irish literature.

Also by Richard J. Finneran

W. B. Yeats, John Sherman and Dhoya (editor)
William Butler Yeats: The Byzantium Poems (editor)
The Prose Fiction of W. B. Yeats: The Search for 'those simple forms'
Letters of James Stephens (editor)
Anglo-Irish Literature: A Review of Research (editor and contributor)
The Correspondence of Robert Bridges and W. B. Yeats (editor)
Letters to W. B. Yeats (co-editor)
The Olympian and the Leprechaun: W. B. Yeats and James Stephens
Some Unpublished Letters from AE to James Stephens (co-editor)
Yeats Annual No. 1 (editor)
Recent Research on Anglo-Irish Writers (editor and contributor)
Yeats Annual No. 2 (editor)

EDITING YEATS'S POEMS

Richard J. Finneran

First edition 1983
Reprinted 1984

Published by
THE MACMILLAN PRESS LTD
London and Basingstoke
Companies and representatives
throughout the world

ISBN 0 333 33966 5

Typeset in Great Britain by
Scarborough Typesetting Services, Yorks
and printed in Great Britain by
Antony Rowe Ltd
Chippenham

'The work is done,' grown old he thought,
'According to my boyish plan;
Let the fools rage, I swerved in nought,
Something to perfection brought';
But louder sang that ghost 'What then?'

Contents

Preface

This study is offered as a companion to *The Poems of W. B. Yeats, a New Edition* (London: Macmillan, 1983). Its purposes are, first, to outline the variety and complexity of the problems encountered in editing Yeats's poems; and, secondly, to explain and to defend the solutions adopted for the new text. This study also suggests that any edition of Yeats's poems will always be a provisional one, partly because not all of the manuscript material will be known or available, partly because many of the editorial decisions will have to be subjective and therefore arguable.

Having worked with Yeats's texts for some years, I remain convinced that the rigorous application to them of any single editorial policy (e.g. always following the last version printed in his lifetime) is inappropriate. This study therefore approaches the problem of editing Yeats's poems through a variety of ways: publication history, textual analysis based on manuscript evidence, critical interpretation, and so on. Though some textual theorists will object to such an eclectic methodology, I hope that by the end of this study I will have been able to demonstrate its appropriateness to the materials at hand.

Any editor of Yeats is conscious of standing on the shoulders of his predecessors. In the present instance, of course, my indebtedness to the late Peter Allt and Russell K. Alspach is immeasurable. Indeed, if their monumental *Variorum Edition of the Poems of W. B. Yeats* (1957) had not been available, it would have had to be done before the present edition could go forward. And their work remains essential for those students interested in Yeats's revisions of his poems.

Any editor of Yeats is also conscious of the collaborative nature of his enterprise. I have acknowledged some specific debts in the footnotes to the present study, and a larger number of individuals are acknowledged in the Preface to the new edition. But if a

complete list could be compiled, it would run to several pages. I
hope that all concerned will accept this general thanks.

I am also indebted to Michael and Anne Yeats for permission to
use both published and unpublished material by Yeats.

Finally, I should like to dedicate this study to Mary, as always.

New Orleans, Louisiana   R. J. F.
24 October 1981

Prolegomena: The Myth of the *Definitive Edition*

Items 209 and 210 in Allan Wade's *A Bibliography of the Writings of W. B. Yeats*, describing the two-volume *Poems* issued by Macmillan, London, in the autumn of 1949, are headed by the magisterial phrase "The Definitive Edition".[1] For reasons that will become clear, I do not believe that a truly "Definitive Edition" of Yeats's poems is or will be possible. I am quite certain, however, that the 1949 *Poems* is defective in contents, in ordering, and in text. As we proceed, I shall therefore also offer my reasons for believing that the new edition of *The Poems of W. B. Yeats*, to which this study is a companion, is a step closer to that archetypal, hence mythical, "Definitive Edition".[2]

The canonisation of *Poems* (1949) began some six years before the edition was published. Writing in *The House of Macmillan (1843–1943)* of the relationship between Yeats and his primary publisher, Charles Morgan explained that

> when a complete edition was projected, his whole works were elaborately studied on his behalf, phrase by phrase and comma by comma, before being submitted to his personal care. The edition has been delayed by the war, but all of it was seen and revised by Yeats. He attended to every point that was raised, explaining his meaning where he thought it might have been missed, and writing: "For the first time there will be a

[1] Allan Wade, *A Bibliography of the Writings of W. B. Yeats*, 3rd ed., rev. Russell K. Alspach (London: Rupert Hart-Davis, 1968), pp. 206–7.
[2] *The Poems of W. B. Yeats, a New Edition*, ed. Richard J. Finneran (London and New York: Macmillan, 1983).

satisfactory text of my work, thanks to your watchfulness and patience."[3]

Despite the hagiographic tone, this description is not altogether an exaggeration: the person referred to in the quotation from Yeats was almost surely Thomas Mark, his principal editor at Macmillan and a man extraordinarily devoted to Yeats's works.[4] Without Mark's dedicated efforts, Yeats's canon would have been in a far worse state than at present; and, given the prevailing attitudes of the time, the 1949 *Poems* was probably as accurate an edition as could have been produced.

The establishment of *Poems* as the "Definitive Edition" rests on the following statement from the Prospectus which accompanied the volumes:

> For some time before his death, W. B. Yeats was engaged in revising the text of this edition of his poems, of which he had corrected the proofs, and for which he had signed the special page to appear at the beginning of Volume I. The outbreak of the Second World War, however, came at a crucial stage in the production of the work, and Messrs. Macmillan & Co. Ltd. had to consider the effects of austere conditions on a publication which had been projected on a lavish scale and which, after the untimely death of this great writer, would have formed a worthy monument to him. It was finally decided that production should be discontinued until after the war, and it is only now, a decade later, that it has become possible to offer the work as it was originally planned.[5]

It must have been apparent to anyone who thought seriously about it that this statement could not be altogether accurate: after all,

---

[3] Charles Morgan, *The House of Macmillan (1843–1943)* (London: Macmillan, 1943), p. 223. I suspect that the quotation is from Yeats's letter of 8 September 1932 to Thomas Mark. See note 4, and Chapter 2, note 13.

[4] As described in *Letters to Macmillan*, ed. Simon Nowell-Smith (London: Macmillan, 1967), p. 22, "Thomas Mark (1890–1963) joined Macmillans in 1913 and, after some years as secretary to the board, was appointed a director in 1944. He retired in 1959, but continued as literary adviser to the firm – and as guide, mentor and friend to many of its authors – until his death". Mark was involved with Yeats's texts as late as the 1962 revised edition of *A Vision*. See my "On Editing Yeats: The Text of *A Vision* (1937)", *Texas Studies in Literature and Language*, 19, No. 1 (Spring 1977), 119–34.

[5] Quoted in *Bibliography*, pp. 207–8.

eleven of the lyrics in the "Last Poems" section had not even been published in Yeats's lifetime. *Poems* does not seem to have been sent for review; but even when virtually the same text appeared a few months later in the *Collected Poems* (1950), no one seems to have objected.[6] In 1956, the American edition of the *Collected Poems* was more or less brought into conformity with *Poems* and was then described as the "definitive edition with the author's final corrections". The canonisation of the 1949 volume was completed a year later, when it was used as the basic text in the monumental *Variorum Edition of the Poems of W. B. Yeats* prepared by Russell K. Alspach and Peter Allt.[7] In the edition itself, Alspach refers to the Prospectus in defending his choice of *Poems* (VP xxix–xxx). As he later explained to me, "Mrs Yeats assured me in conversation that the 1949 two-volume edition fully warranted the word 'definitive': that WBY had corrected the proof and arranged the poems in the order he wanted. She clearly implied that his were the final corrections".[8]

Sadly, this was something less than the full truth, and Mrs Yeats knew that it was. But it was left to Curtis Bradford to begin the process of questioning the authority of the 1949 *Poems*. In an essay published in 1961, Bradford reproduced a manuscript table of contents which suggested that the contents and order of the Cuala Press *Last Poems and Two Plays* (1939) was to be preferred over that of the Macmillan *Last Poems & Plays* (1940).[9] He elaborated and extended that argument in a monograph on *Yeats's 'Last Poems' Again* (1966).[10] My own research, drawing on material unavailable to Bradford (such as the Macmillan Archive in the British Library), has not only confirmed Bradford's suspicions

---

[6] *The Collected Poems* (London: Macmillan, 1950; New York: Macmillan, 1951) prints "The Fool by the Roadside" in place of "The Hero, the Girl, and the Fool" found in *Poems* (1949). The explanation for this discrepancy will be given in Chapter 2. There are also some other minor differences between the two editions in the Notes.

[7] *The Variorum Edition of the Poems of W. B. Yeats*, ed. Peter Allt and Russell K. Alspach (New York: Macmillan, 1957). The corrected third printing of 1966 hereafter cited VP.

[8] Letter from Russell K. Alspach to Richard J. Finneran, 30 September 1976.

[9] Curtis Bradford, "The Order of *Last Poems*", *Modern Language Notes*, 76, No. 6 (June 1961), 515–16.

[10] Curtis Bradford, *Yeats's 'Last Poems' Again*, Dolmen Press Yeats Centenary Papers, No. 8 (Dublin: Dolmen Press, 1966). Stanley Sultan's *Yeats at His Last*, Dolmen Press New Yeats Papers, No. 11 (Dublin: Dolmen Press, 1975) reasserts Bradford's thesis but offers little new evidence.

about *Last Poems* but also discovered other defects in the "Definitive Edition" of 1949. The basic problem with *Poems* is that for most of the works included it uses as its source some proofs on which Yeats last worked in 1932, ignoring the decisions which he thereafter made for the 1933 *Collected Poems*. Thus we must now turn to the sometimes melancholy story of the unpublished Macmillan "Edition de Luxe".

CHAPTER ONE

The Edition de Luxe

By 1926 Yeats's works had already been the subject of two collected editions: the eight volumes of the sumptuous *Collected
Works in Verse & Prose* issued by the Shakespeare Head Press in
1908; and the more mundane series of six volumes issued by Macmillan over a period of five years (*Later Poems*, 1922; *Plays in
Prose and Verse*, 1922; *Plays and Controversies*, 1923; *Essays*,
1924; *Early Poems and Stories*, 1925; *Autobiographies*, 1926).
The latter series, though, was something of a putative collected
edition. The title "The Collected Works of W. B. Yeats" appears
only in the final two volumes — and only at the end of each book.
And of course the gathering was incomplete, the 1925 *A Vision*
being the most notable exclusion.

Indeed, the publication of a collected edition by Macmillan had
been a point of some dissension between Yeats and his publisher
for several years. In a letter of 27 June 1916, A. P. Watt (Yeats's
literary agent) wrote to Macmillan that Yeats accepted their offer
for "the publication of a new edition of his collected works, and
the transfer of the existing stock of certain of his books from Mr.
A. H. Bullen to yourselves".[1] But instead of a Collected Works, the
first books published by Macmillan, London, after the agreement
were *Reveries Over Childhood & Youth* (1916), *Responsibilities*
(1916), *Per Amica Silentia Lunae* (1918), *The Wild Swans at
Coole* (1919), and *The Cutting of an Agate* (1919). Thus on 30
October 1919 Watt passed on to Sir Frederick Macmillan Yeats's

---

[1] British Library, Additional Manuscripts 54897, f. 193. References to British
Library manuscripts will be hereafter provided in the text, on the model of
manuscript number/folio number(s). The Macmillan Archive in the British
Library has been described by William E. Fredeman, "The Bibliographical
Significance of a Publisher's Archive: The Macmillan Papers", *Studies in
Bibliography*, 23 (1970), 183–91; and by Philip V. Blake-Hill, "The Mac-
millan Archive", *British Museum Quarterly*, 36, Nos. 3–4 (Autumn 1972),
74–80.

recommendation that they "publish now some part of their proposed uniform edition of my works" (54898/44). After further correspondence, by early 1920 the publishers were willing to undertake some three volumes. Yeats was clearly dissatisfied, and on 20 January 1922 Watt sent Macmillan a forceful reminder that "the formal agreement between your Firm and Mr. Yeats, dated June 27th 1916, provides for the publication of a Collected Edition in not less than six volumes" (54898/138). It was doubtless that letter which spurred on Macmillan to begin the publication of the six-volume series the following autumn.

Macmillan's reluctance to undertake a collected works was certainly not caused by their inexperience in the genre. Over the years they had published numerous such editions, including twenty-six volumes by Henry James (1907–17), five volumes by William Ernest Henley (1921), fifteen volumes by John Morley (1921), and twenty volumes by Eden Phillpotts (1927–28). More to the point is Charles Morgan's explanation that "the times were not propitious for the issue of collected and limited editions. . . . The only real success was the Mellstock Hardy in thirty-seven volumes".[2] The Yeats series, however, did achieve some impressive sales figures: the 1500 copies of *Later Poems* were exhausted within a month of publication, and there were further impressions in December 1922, February 1924, and March 1926. None of the other volumes required a second impression, but by the time of *Early Poems and Stories* the print-order had nearly doubled to 2908 copies. It may be that by the beginning of 1930 the sales figures had made Macmillan receptive to the concept of a Collected Works more in accord with Yeats's expectations as well as his past publishing history; or it may be Yeats and his agent maintained pressure for such an edition. In any event, it is clear that when publisher and agent met sometime between 1 and 10 February 1930, one of the topics discussed, as Macmillan later wrote to Watt, was "the possibility of our acquiring the rights to Early Poems from Benn, with a view to the subsequent publication of an edition de luxe" (55704/195).

The discussions between Watt and Macmillan about the Edition de Luxe continued throughout 1930, one of the problems indeed being the acquisition by Ernest Benn a few years earlier of the

---

[2] *The House of Macmillan*, p. 226. The Hardy edition was published in 1921–22.

rights to the much-revised *Poems*.[3] On 11 February 1930, Macmillan objected to the publication of a limited American edition of *Oedipus at Colonus* "especially if we are going seriously to consider having a complete edition de luxe of all Mr. Yeats's works" (55695/571).[4] On 17 March 1930, Macmillan told Watt that "if we could clear away some of these difficulties, we could proceed with the more important plan of a new collected edition. This, however, must be held up until the smaller matters have been disposed of" (55697/360). The first news that Yeats had of the Edition de Luxe may have come in a letter from Macmillan on 5 September 1930, in which he was urged to contact Watt about several matters under discussion, including "the tentative proposals which we have made for a new, collected, limited edition de luxe for all your work" (55704/582). On 4 October 1930 Macmillan sent Watt a long letter about the project with some specific suggestions, including the proposal that Yeats withhold his current work for initial publication in the Edition de Luxe (55706/136−8). On 12 December 1930, Watt sent Macmillan a typed copy of a letter from Yeats with various queries about the Edition (54901/102−3). Two days later Watt forwarded a copy of a second letter from Yeats, in which he wondered if the Edition could include a book which he had planned to propose to Macmillan in 1931. This was to include *A Vision* (1925), *Estrangement* (1926), *The Death of Synge* (1928), *A Packet for Ezra Pound* (1929), and *Stories of Michael Robartes and His Friends* (1932). Yeats explained that

> these four sections support each other. 'A Vision' is not the crude book published by Laurie; I have worked years on it since then. The philosophic stories, which were written this summer and are amongst the best things I have written, expound its

[3] In an inscription in his copy of *Poems* (London: Ernest Benn, [1929]), quoted in *Bibliography*, pp. 156−7, Yeats lamented that "this book for about thirty years brought me twenty or thirty times as much money as any other book of mine − no twenty or thirty times as much as all my other books put together. This success was pure accident. Five or six years ago 'T. Fisher Unwin' ceased to exist and it passed to the firm of 'Benn' & within twelve months the sales were halved, & another twelve months fallen to one tenth of what they had been." Yeats's dissatisfaction with Benn was one of the reasons behind his desire for a *Collected Poems*.

[4] In a letter of 20 February 1932, Yeats recalled that he had "passed the last proof" of that edition. *The Letters of W. B. Yeats*, ed. Allan Wade (London: Rupert Hart-Davis, 1954), p. 792. Hereafter cited L.

fundamental ideas. "A Packet for Ezra Pound" is the introduction to "A Vision" and the "Diaries" which are probably my best critical writings have sufficient relation to it not to seem out of harmony. I don't want to publish "A Vision" by itself for various reasons. (54901/104)

Macmillan responded to Watt on 12 December 1930, indicating that he indeed wanted the Edition to be complete and that it could probably not be published until the spring of 1932 (55709/446–8). In Yeats's mind the question was settled: he told Olivia Shakespear on 27 December 1930 that "Macmillan are going to bring out an Edition de Luxe of all my work published and unpublished. . . . I am to be ready next autumn at latest. Months of re-writing. What happiness!" (L 780). The Edition was arranged in a more formal way when Watt wrote to Macmillan on 15 January 1931, stating that "I have heard from Mr. Yeats and he accepts your offer and approves the specimen page" (54901/114). The actual agreement for the Edition was sent by Macmillan to Watt on 20 April 1931 (55715/241) and returned signed by Yeats on 4 May 1931 (54901/160).

Yeats wasted no time in setting to work. He wrote to Macmillan from Killiney on 7 May to inquire about the number of pages in the extant collected edition: "As soon as I get these numbers of pages I will send you a suggested list for the contents of the different volumes in the edition de luxe of my work which you are bringing out. I shall be going to England in about ten days and shall hope to bring you the contents of five or six of the seven volumes" (55003/121). Yeats fulfilled his promise when he met with Harold Macmillan at 11:00 a.m. on 1 June 1931 (54901/171). Shortly thereafter he told an interviewer that

I've just finished the *de luxe* edition of my works that Macmillan is bringing out. I deposited on his floor the other day six of the seven volumes. I'm now going back to Ireland to get the seventh. The seventh volume is entirely philosophical, with a small amount of fantastic romance.[5]

Nor did Macmillan delay long in putting the Edition de Luxe into production. As one would expect, *Poems* was the first volume

---

[5] Louise Morgan, *Writers at Work* (London: Chatto & Windus, 1931), pp. 8–9. The British Library copy of the volume was received on 16 September 1931, so the interview must have taken place at this time.

to be printed. Galley proofs were prepared on 12 September 1931. These must have been for in-house use only, as the first set of page proofs was printed on 18 September 1931. Very little of this material is known to survive: most of what is extant is in the collection of Michael B. Yeats, though there are two galleys in the National Library of Ireland.[6] I do not know why the page proofs were not sent to Yeats in the autumn of 1931. Certainly Yeats was preoccupied at the time with the terminally ill Lady Gregory: as he wrote L. A. G. Strong on 4 December 1931, "I am staying at Coole Park . . . the family has asked me to be there as much as I can at present. I come up to Dublin only for Abbey business and never stay more than two or three days, and my wife looks through my correspondence and puts such letters as I must attend to myself on my table" (L 787). On the other hand, the changing economic conditions may have been giving the publishers second thoughts: Yeats told James Sullivan Starkey on 20 February 1932 that Macmillan "is about to publish 'an edition de luxe' of my work, when the depression has moved off . . ." (L 792). For whatever reason, there seems to have been no progress on *Poems* until Yeats met with Macmillan on 13 April 1932 and promised to "send us some new poems for this volume, which are to be inserted after the 'Byzantium' section" (55727/271).[7] Yeats submitted the new matter and proceeded to inquire twice about the whereabouts of the proofs. On 17 June 1932, Macmillan forwarded to him "a complete marked set of proofs of Volume I (Poems) of the Edition de Luxe of your works, together with the printed pages and other material which you supplied us for use as 'copy'" (55729/477). On 22 June 1932, Macmillan also sent the proofs of *Mythologies* (55729/605).

Yeats, now in Dublin after the death of Lady Gregory on 22 May

[6] In National Library of Ireland MS. 13,589.

[7] In the autumn of 1930 Yeats was planning to bring out a volume first called *The Winding Stair* and later *Byzantium*. The contents would have included the poems from *The Winding Stair* (New York: Fountain Press, [1929]) as well as some new work, including the poem "Byzantium". See *W. B. Yeats and T. Sturge Moore: Their Correspondence, 1901–1937*, ed. Ursula Bridge (London: Routledge & Kegan Paul, 1953), pp. 163–6. On 5 January 1931 Yeats wrote Moore that "there will be delay over *Byzantium*. Macmillan proposes to bring out an *édition de luxe* of all my works, including it, before the edition with your cover comes out. This will follow after one month. I say I shall have my work in *édition de luxe* finished in time for autumnal publication. Macmillan says I wont. His general knowledge of authors may be sounder than my particular knowledge of myself" (p. 166). It was.

1932, had told H. J. C. Grierson on 9 June 1932 that "my summer will be spent over proof sheets: my own new collected edition" (L 797), and he was true to his word as regards *Poems* and *Mythologies*. On 30 June 1932, almost two weeks after he had received the proofs of *Poems*, he wrote Olivia Shakespear that "I spend my days correcting proofs. I have just finished the first volume, all my lyric poetry . . ." and went on to make the oft-quoted statement that "the swordsman throughout repudiates the saint, but not without vacillation" (L 798). On 5 July 1932 Yeats wrote to Macmillan to say that he was returning the two sets of proofs. In his response, Macmillan noted that "you do not wish to see 'Mythologies' (Vol. II) again, though you would like to have a revise of the whole of the volume of poems. We shall be sending you proofs of the remaining volumes before you leave Ireland early in October" (55730/301). When Yeats failed to receive the revised proofs, he wrote on 13 August 1932 explaining the reason for his request:

> You would still further add to my indebtedness to you if you would let me have a revise of volume one of the collected edition de luxe, or at any rate of everything in that volume after "The Tower". I had marked it "revise" when I sent in the proofs and I want the latter part now so that I may get a book of verse together for the Macmillan Company and so protect my American copyrights. I made corrections in the poems of which I have kept no copies, and there are notes which I want. (55003/135)

On 23 August 1932 Macmillan was able to send Yeats pp. 1–384 of *Poems*, explaining that "the remainder of this volume has yet to reach us from the printers" (55731/569). This marked set of proofs survives in the collection of Michael B. Yeats; the first 384 pages bear date-stamps from 22 July to 3 August 1932. On 16 September 1932 Macmillan was at last able to forward the missing proofs of *Poems* (55732/366). Yeats returned these proofs on 28 September 1932 and asked for "a 'revise' of these pages soon, as I start for America on Oct 21 & the nearer I come to the date the busier I shall be" (55003/138). Macmillan complied with this request, sending the proofs for pp. 385ff. to the printers on 30 September 1932.[8] The revised proofs, also in the collection of Michael B. Yeats, bear the date-stamp of 4 October 1932.

[8] Information from the "Printers" books in the archives of Macmillan, London, in Basingstoke, vol. 32, f. 9.

Since our concern is with the poems, there is no need to trace in any detail the later history of the Edition de Luxe.[9] Were we to do so, we would find a tale with three main strands: (1) the sporadic but continual production and correction of galley and page proofs; (2) the constant postponement of publication, for a variety of reasons; and (3) the slow accretion of the project, until it reached an eventual total of eleven volumes. Beginning in November 1935, its history is also tied up with the never-published Scribner Edition, a story in itself.[10] After Yeats's death, the title Edition de Luxe was changed to "The Coole Edition", a name suggested by Mrs Yeats.[11] The apogee of the Coole Edition occurred in the summer of 1939, when a full-page advertisement in the special Yeats issue of *The Arrow* announced publication, in the full glory of eleven volumes, "this Autumn". But the shadow of world events overtook even the best of intentions, and on 19 October 1939 Mark wrote to Mrs Yeats that the Coole Edition "has to wait for better times" (55830/334). On 24 November 1939, the publishers informed Arthur Duff, who had been assisting with the printing of some music, that "owing to the war the publication of the Coole edition has been suspended . . ." (55003/269).

But even though the Coole Edition was never to be published, its effect on Yeats's texts was far-reaching. We turn now to the first of its offshoots, *The Collected Poems* of 1933.

---

[9] For more information on the Edition de Luxe, see the Introduction to *The Secret Rose, Stories by W. B. Yeats: A Variorum Edition*, ed. Phillip L. Marcus, Warwick Gould, and Michael J. Sidnell (Ithaca and London: Cornell University Press, 1981), pp. xvii–xxix. Gould is preparing a detailed history of the Edition.

[10] For information on the Scribner Edition, see Edward Callan, *Yeats on Yeats: The Last Introductions and the 'Dublin' Edition*, New Yeats Papers, No. 20 (Dublin: Dolmen Press, 1981), esp. pp. 87–103.

[11] On 28 February 1939, Harold Macmillan told Mrs Yeats that "I think that the edition ought, if possible, to be given some appropriate name (like the Sussex Edition of Kipling's works), and I wonder if you have any ideas on that point" (55820/205). Mark repeated the request on 14 April 1939 (55882/342). Mrs Yeats replied to Mark the following day, stating "I suggest THE *COOLE* EDITION as name. He owed so much to Lady Gregory that this title would commemorate" (carbon in the collection of Michael B. Yeats; the original is missing from the file of correspondence at Macmillan, London). On 19 April 1939, Harold Macmillan wrote to Watt that "I like the idea of calling the new edition The Coole Edition, and we are adopting that title. Scribner's is called the Dublin Edition" (55882/452).

CHAPTER TWO

The Winding Stair and Other Poems and The Collected Poems

Yeats was in London from "about Oct 8" 1932 until he left for his American lecture tour on 21 October 1932 (L 802). As we have seen, he had with him a complete set of corrected page proofs for the Edition de Luxe *Poems*. I conjecture that Yeats met with his publishers on 19 or 20 October 1932. Among other things, he would have been seeking assurances that there would be no further delays in publishing the Edition de Luxe and that it would indeed appear in the spring of 1933, as Macmillan had suggested to him in a letter of 11 August 1932 (55731/405–7). When such assurances were not forthcoming, I believe that Yeats made a counter proposal: why not go ahead and publish *Poems* immediately in a trade edition, a *Collected Poems*? By the time the Edition de Luxe was ready to go forward, Yeats would have further poems to add to the collection, so that the publisher's desire for new material in the Edition would be met. Moreover, the agreement with Ernest Benn was to expire in May 1933 (54902/4), and no new book of Yeats's poems had been published in London since *The Tower* (1928). Yeats must have been convincing, as on 20 October 1932 Macmillan wrote to Watt about "a new proposal which Mr. Yeats has made to me" (55733/424).

On the other side of the Atlantic, Yeats carried his suggestion to George P. Brett, Jr., of the New York Macmillan Company, meeting with him probably in late December 1932. In a letter exhibiting both his diplomacy and his shrewd business sense, Yeats wrote to Macmillan on 22 December 1932 that Brett "will be writing to you in a day or two about the proposed issue of my lyric poems in one volume. He proposed such a volume to me without knowing that you had the same idea" (55003/139).[1] Yeats's letter

---

[1] This communication must have occurred, but I have been unable to find any such letter in the British Library file of correspondence from George P. Brett, Jr., to Macmillan, London (Additional Manuscripts 54855).

produced the desired effect: on 5 January 1933, Macmillan replied to him that he had sent the proofs of the Edition de Luxe to Brett and that "I shall look forward to hearing from him about the proposed issue of your lyric poems in one volume" (55736/105). At the same time, Macmillan inquired from Watt if any unforeseen difficulties had arisen with Ernest Benn (55736/104). After further correspondence and reassurances from Watt that Benn was agreeable (albeit reluctantly) to the project, Macmillan asked Watt on 18 February 1933 "May I take it that you agree, and that everything is now ready for the preparation of our complete edition of the poems?" Macmillan also wanted to know the date of Yeats's return from America, as "there are also one or two points about the arrangement of the poems which I should like to discuss with him" (55737/291). Yeats was in fact already back in Dublin, having passed through London on 27 January 1933 (L 804).

On 13 March 1933, Macmillan wrote to Watt, stating definitely that "I now wish to proceed with the project for the complete edition of Mr. Yeats' poems in one volume" and that "we should propose to follow the contents that have already been decided upon for the Edition de luxe". Macmillan also reminded Watt that "I do not know whether Mr. Yeats wishes to see a specimen page or whether he has any views about the arrangement . . ." (55738/97). Watt passed on these queries to Yeats. Yeats replied directly to Macmillan on 17 March 1933, in a letter to have a significant effect on the later history of his texts. After explaining that he need not see a specimen page but would require proofs, Yeats asked an important question:

> Would you advise me, or ask the accomplished reader of yours to advise me on one point. In Vol I of the Edition de Luxe I think I included the dramatic poem "The Shadowy Waters" on the ground that it is not a stage-play but a poem (there is a stage version among my dramatic works), should it be included in the present book? This question decided one way or the other please follow the contents of Vol I of the edition de Luxe. I probably put some sentence in a preface or note to account for the presence of the dramatic poem. If "The Shadowy Waters" is left out I will of course alter this. (55003/140)

Yeats had doubtless anticipated the "one or two points about the arrangement of the poems" which were already in his publisher's

mind. Macmillan replied on 30 March 1933. After apologising for
the delay, he made the following suggestion:

> As regards the contents of the volume, I share our reader's view
> that it would be a pity to omit "The Shadowy Waters". There is,
> however, one departure from the arrangement of the Edition de
> Luxe volume which I should like to put before you, as it has been
> suggested by more than one person. We think it possible that the
> book would be more attractive to the potential purchaser who
> glances through it in a bookshop if what first caught his eye were
> the shorter lyrical poems contained in "Crossways", "The Rose",
> "The Wind Among the Reeds", etc., rather than a lengthy work
> like "The Wanderings of Oisin". Our impression is that we
> might move the longer narrative and dramatic pieces to the end
> of the volume, where they would make a group more or less
> related in style, subject, and length, and I wonder if you would
> agree to our taking this course with the following longer
> works:—
>
> "The Wanderings of Oisin"
> "The Old Age of Queen Maeve"
> "Baile and Ailinn"
> "The Shadowy Waters"
> and "The Two Kings"
>
> If this arrangement commends itself to you, and if you could
> think of some general title we could use to cover this particular
> group, I will instruct the printers to proceed with the work on
> those lines. Needless to say, however, the suggestion is quite
> tentative, and we should not wish to do anything of the kind
> without your full approval. (55003/460−2)[2]

Yeats replied almost at once. He wrote Macmillan on 2 April 1933
that

> I am delighted with your suggestion to put long poems in a
> section at the end. I wish I had thought of it before.
> You could call this group "longer poems", & the rest of the

---

[2] This letter is included in *Letters to W. B. Yeats*, ed. Richard J. Finneran,
George Mills Harper, and William M. Murphy (London: Macmillan, 1977),
p. 552.

book "shorter poems", or you could call this group "Narrative and dramatic poetry["], & the rest of book "lyrical poetry." (55003/141)

The publishers replied on 10 April 1933, expressing their delight at Yeats's decision and choosing the second set of suggested titles for the sections (55739/55–6).

I have quoted this exchange of letters at such length because of the monumental textual discrepancy which it created. That is, in the Collected Poems, the works listed in Macmillan's letter, along with "The Gift of Harun Al-Rashid", were indeed placed at the rear of the book, in a section called "Narrative and Dramatic"; the book opens with a section called "Lyrical". On the other hand, the "Definitive Edition" of Poems (1949) reverts to the interspersed format used on the 1932 proofs for the Edition de Luxe Poems; thus it, as well as the Variorum Poems, opens not with "The Song of the Happy Shepherd" but with "The Wanderings of Oisin" and thereafter presents all of Yeats's poems in a roughly chronological scheme.

It is clear that what we are offered here is not merely two different "arrangements", but two different incarnations of the archetypal "Sacred Book" of the poems, thus two different experiences of reading Yeats and of attempting to come to terms with his massive achievement. Which plan is in fact Yeats's "final intention"?

On the one hand, it is possible to argue that Yeats was simply agreeing to his publisher's suggestion in order to increase his earnings on the collection. Moreover, since at the time he still anticipated the eventual publication of the Edition de Luxe, he could take comfort in the fact that his poems would later appear in the preferred arrangement.[3] It is also difficult to believe that a writer who had been arranging and rearranging his poems at least since the 1895 Poems should have "not thought of" the generic division before it was suggested to him.

[3] Such is the view of Harold Macmillan, as reported by Warwick Gould in a letter to Richard J. Finneran on 22 September 1980. According to Gould, Macmillan "remembered the suggestion of re-ordering the Collected Poems as being 'Mark's suggestion,' but felt that such a suggestion was for a book to be 'sold' whilst the 'canonical' edition was in process, and could not see such a provisional decision as revising the ordering agreed on for the canonical volumes . . . but as something done to aid sales of a volume which had no 'memorial' standing."

On the other hand, it is possible to argue that Yeats was never given to placing his finances before his art. Moreover, it may well be that both Yeats and his publishers recognised that — with the arguable exceptions of "The Wanderings of Oisin" and "The Shadowy Waters" — the narrative and dramatic poems were not among Yeats's best and should be placed so as not to distract from his essentially lyrical achievement.[4] It might also be suggested that the twofold division of the collection accords with Yeats's sense of antithesis as the dominant characteristic of reality.

In weighing the available evidence about this issue, one should bear in mind not only what Yeats did but also what he did *not* do. That is, he did not respond to Macmillan to the effect that the order might be changed for the *Collected Poems* but must remain as planned for the Edition de Luxe; he did not write to Olivia Shakespear or some other correspondent likely to preserve his letters and express displeasure at the format of the 1933 volume; nor did he inscribe his own copy of the *Collected Poems* with a note regretting the order of the poems. Perhaps most crucially, when in late 1935 he agreed to the publication of the Scribner Edition, he did not request a return to the Edition de Luxe format but specifically instructed the publishers that "Poems should be taken from COLLECTED POEMS (London edition)".[5]

We will of course never know what Yeats might have done if the Edition de Luxe had gone forward in 1935, when he had the lyrics from *A Full Moon in March* to add; in 1938, when he also had *New Poems* to add; or in 1939, when he also had *Last Poems* to insert. He might, for instance, have concluded that the lack of a long poem since "Harun Al-Rashid" made the 1932 plan no longer tenable. Or he might well have abandoned all thought of the earlier format because of his satisfaction with the *Collected Poems* division. What we are left with, then, is the existence of Yeats's

[4] The chronology of the composition of the later narrative poems suggests that Yeats felt compelled to experiment with the genre every few years, even though (or because?) he was never fully successful with it.

[5] Yeats as quoted by H. Watt in a letter to George P. Brett, Jr., 3 December 1935, in Callan, *Yeats on Yeats*, p. 91. The letter of agreement from Brett to Charles Scribner, dated 8 October 1936, also indicates "that you agree to take the poems from COLLECTED POEMS (London edition)" (Callan, p. 93).

Although, as we shall see in the next chapter, Macmillan, London was anxious that there should be as much divergence as possible between the Edition de Luxe and the Scribner Edition, they were hardly in a position to object if Yeats had decided to use the Edition de Luxe order for the Scribner volume of poems.

letter to Macmillan of 2 April 1933 and the fact that after he agreed to the revised order he made some important changes (to be discussed later in this chapter) in the contents and order of "The Tower" section of the volume. I have therefore chosen to follow the arrangement of the *Collected Poems* in the new edition of *Poems*.

To continue the narrative of the *Collected Poems* is to turn now to *The Winding Stair and Other Poems*. On 28 June 1933 Macmillan sent Yeats the proofs of the *Collected Poems* but went on to suggest a new volume:

> I notice that the "Collected Poems" contains the text of "The Winding Stair and Other Poems" which has not been issued in separate form, except, I understand, by the Cuala Press. My partners and I would be glad if we could arrange to publish this work as a separate volume, probably in the same style as "The Tower", which is somewhat similar in length. It would clearly be advantageous to publish it in this form before the volume of "Collected Poems" is issued, and, if you agree, we will set it up at once from your corrected proofs of the "Collected Poems" and issue it, say, in September, postponing the "Collected Poems" until November. (55741/386−7)

Harold Macmillan may have been a bit deficient in bibliographical information − the Cuala Press had published only that portion of the section included in *Words for Music Perhaps* (1932) − but he had a good eye for the market. Yeats accepted the proposal the very next day (55003/144) and presumably began correcting the proofs. On 13 July 1933 Macmillan inquired as to the state of the proofs (55742/162); Yeats must have returned them at once, as on 15 July 1933 Thomas Mark wrote "to acknowledge with thanks the receipt of the corrected page proofs of your Collected Poems. We will see that a revise reaches you in due course" (55742/196).

On 2 August 1933 Macmillan was able to forward the "marked page proofs of "The Winding Stair" in its separate form, together with the proofs of the section of the "Collected Poems" from which it has been set up". A suggestion was made about the arrangement of the titles in the "Words for Music Perhaps" section, and a plea was added that Yeats deal with the proofs "as quickly as possible"

(55742/543). Yeats complied again, and the proofs were back with the publishers by 9 August 1933 (55743/19). In the accompanying letter Yeats justified his arrangement:

> Please leave the section called "Words for Music Perhaps" as I have arranged[,] every poem with its number. It is a series of poems related one to another & leads up to a question from the Delphic oracle, as the two other series "A Man Young & Old" and "A Woman Young & Old" lead up to quotations from Sophocles. The poems in "Words for Music Perhaps" describe first wild loves, then the normal love of boy & girl, then follow poems about love but not love poems, then poems of impersonal ecstasy, & all have certain themes in common.

Yeats added that "if your admirable reader will see a revised proof of "The Winding Stair" you need not send me another proof. He seems able to read my difficult writing" (55003/147).

Thomas Mark undertook that task, and *The Winding Stair and Other Poems* was published without further revision on 19 September 1933, in an edition of 2000 copies: what most readers consider one of the two finest volumes in Yeats's career the result of a publisher's request.

Yeats wrote to Macmillan on 21 or 22 September 1933 to ask for an errata slip to correct the misprint "yellow canvas" for "swelling canvas" in "Old Tom Again" (55003/150). Macmillan replied that they would insert an errata slip "in all the unsold copies" (55744/358). On 27 September 1933 Macmillan sent to Yeats "a revise of the complete page proofs of your "Collected Poems", together with the set bearing your original corrections" (55744/395). Yeats must have returned these proofs by Saturday, 30 September 1933, as they were in the hands of Macmillan by the next Monday (55744/541). On 1 October 1933, however, Yeats discovered an unnoticed mistake in the Notes to *The Winding Stair*: by "a slip of the pen" he had written, in reference to "The Mother of God", that "She conceived of the Word, and therefore through the ear a star fell and was born"; the intended reading was "She received the Word through the ear, a star fell, and a star was born". Yeats pleaded for the correction or at least an errata slip, "otherwise the error will hand me over to the clerical enemy" (55003/152). An errata slip correcting both "Old Tom Again" and the Notes was inserted into the unsold copies of *The Winding*

Stair;[6] both corrections were made in the text of the *Collected Poems*. At last, the *Collected Poems* was published in London on 28 November 1933, in an edition of 2040 copies; the American edition, set from the corrected proofs of the English volume, had appeared two weeks previously.[7]

We must now look again at the corrected page proofs of *The Winding Stair and Other Poems*. Fortunately, these survive, bearing date-stamps of 2 July–2 August 1933, in the British Library (Add. Mss. 55878). As was usual at this time, the process of correcting the proofs was essentially one of collaboration between Thomas Mark and Yeats, Mark making suggestions and Yeats accepting or rejecting them as well as adding his own revisions.

These proofs are of considerable interest in themselves, as Yeats always treated a proof as simply another stage in the process of composition. It is only here, for instance, that he was able to change ll. 65–6 of "A Dialogue of Self and Soul" from "Content to trace that misery to its source, / Count every sin of action or of thought" to "I am content to follow to its source / Every event in action or in thought". But the most fascinating example of revision concerns the final stanza of "Crazy Jane and Jack the Journeyman".

As printed in *Words for Music Perhaps*, which was finished by the Cuala Press "in the last week of September 1932", the stanza read:

> But were I left to lie alone
> In an empty bed—
> The skein so bound us ghost to ghost

---

[6] The errata slip is not noted in *Bibliography*, pp. 172–3, and the *Variorum Poems* treats the misprints as variants (pp. 530, 832). I discovered the errata slip in James Stephens's copy of *The Winding Stair and Other Poems*, now in my possession, and noted its existence in *The Olympian and the Leprechaun: W. B. Yeats and James Stephens*, New Yeats Papers, No. 16 (Dublin: Dolmen Press, 1978), p. 30.

[7] For the use of the English proofs by the American publishers, see the letters from Macmillan, London, to Macmillan, New York, in British Library Additional Manuscripts 55306, f. 422, and 55307, ff. 11–12, 49, 64, 119, and 130. It is interesting to note that on 24 November 1933, Macmillan, London, objected to having Yeats sign 500 copies of the American *Winding Stair* as "an important edition de luxe is now in the press, and we think that Mr. Yeats should keep any signed edition off the market until the time comes" (55307/204).

> When you turned your head
> Passing on the road that night—
> Mine would walk, being dead.[8]

Richard Ellmann's dating of the poem as written in November
1931 is confirmed by its absence from the 12 September 1931
galley proofs of the Edition de Luxe; nor would it have been on the
18 September 1931 in-house page proofs, the relevant portion of
which has not survived.[9] Thus we cannot be certain of the reading
on the 7 September 1932 first page proofs or the 16 September
1932 second page proofs. But by the time of the 4 October 1932
revised page proofs, the stanza read as follows:

> But were I left to lie alone
> In an empty bed;
> The skein so bound my ghost and his
> When he turned his head about
> Passing on the road that night
> Mine must walk when dead.

On one set of these page proofs (which Yeats apparently prepared
as copy for *The Winding Stair and Other Poems*, possibly thinking
it might be required for the American edition), the stanza was
revised to

> But were I left to lie alone
> In an empty bed;
> The skein so bound my ghost and his
> When he turned his head,
> Passing on the road that night,
> Mine must walk when dead.

Unfortunately, I have been unable to locate any proof materials
for the 1933 *Collected Poems*.[10] However, I suspect that the poem
would have appeared on them in this form. In any case, it was so
printed on the proofs of *The Winding Stair and Other Poems*
which Yeats received.

---

[8] *Words for Music Perhaps and Other Poems* (Dublin: Cuala Press, 1932), p. 26.
[9] Richard Ellmann, *The Identity of Yeats*, 2nd ed. (London: Faber and Faber,
   1964), p. 292.
[10] The last known reference to these proofs is the letter from Macmillan to Yeats
   on 2 October 1933, acknowledging "the parcel containing the proofs of the
   volume of 'Collected Poems' passed for press" (55744/541).

Yeats was dissatisfied with this version — in particular, he had lost the interlocking slant rime "lost"/"ghost" (cf. "unwound"/ "ground") — and on *The Winding Stair* proofs he decided to combine some aspects of the intermediate text with the final line from the earliest version:

> But were I left to lie alone
> In an empty bed,
> The skein so bound us ghost to ghost
> When he turned his head
> Passing on the road that night,
> Mine would walk being dead.

But the 1949 *Poems* uses another revision of the 1932 page proofs; this is identical with *The Winding Stair* text except that the final line remains "Mine must walk when dead". The substitution seems a clear example of the losses incurred when the Edition de Luxe proofs are preferred over the later texts of *The Winding Stair* and the *Collected Poems*. To demonstrate that assertion we must glance briefly at the poem as a whole.

"Crazy Jane and Jack the Journeyman" is a complex lyric, especially until we recall a statement Yeats made to Louise Morgan in 1931: "'If you don't express yourself,' he said, 'you walk after you're dead. The great thing is to go empty to your grave.'"[11] Central to the poem, in which Jane is trying both to understand and to justify love, particularly sexual love, is the traditional dual meaning of "ghost" as "the soul or spirit, as the principle of life" and "the soul of a deceased person" (OED). In the first stanza Jane recognises the inherent transiency of all love and comes to understand that in some ways it is that very transiency which gives love its ultimate value: "For love is but a skein unwound / Between the dark and the dawn". In the opening lines of the next stanza Jane

---

[11] *Writers at Work*, p. 9. Previous commentators seem to have overlooked the relevance of Yeats's statement to the poem. Thomas Parkinson, *W. B. Yeats: The Later Poetry* (Berkeley and Los Angeles: University of California Press, 1964), pp. 211–16, offers an interesting discussion of the manuscripts. The readings by John Unterecker in *A Reader's Guide to William Butler Yeats* (New York: Noonday Press, 1959), pp. 227–8, and Harold Bloom in *Yeats* (New York: Oxford University Press, 1970), p. 401, are similar but, I think, wrong. My interpretation follows in some respects Laurence Perrine, "Yeats's 'Crazy Jane and Jack the Journeyman'", *CEA Critic*, 34, No. 3 (March 1972), 22–3.

admits that human love does not survive the death of the body, that after death one journeys in solitude: "A lonely ghost the ghost is / That to God shall come". In one sense, then, Jane will eventually become such a "lonely ghost"; but as long as she continues to live, her ghost in the sense of soul has surely *not* been lonely. She thus believes that the complete self-expression which she can achieve through love in this life will enable her to circumvent God's judgment after death and to enter a heaven which is less Christian than Platonic. "Love's skein upon the ground," she can "leap into the light lost / In my mother's womb." The central contrast is between "shall come" and "shall leap".

In the final stanza Jane steps back to consider the alternative. Had she denied the intense love which she felt for Jack on their first encounter, her journey towards full self-expression would have been frustrated; and after death she would find herself not in the "light" but in the darkness of a Yeatsian Purgatory, attempting to accomplish in a discarnate state what she had failed to accomplish in life. Moreover, if she were even *now* to find herself "alone / In an empty bed", if, that is, she were to remain faithful to "my dear Jack that's dead", the result would be the same: love and existence must be conterminous. "Mine would walk being dead" is thus both literal and metaphorical: a denial of love would cause both the physically dead ghost ("soul of a deceased person") and the symbolically dead ghost ("soul or spirit, as the principle of life") to "walk" in search of what had been denied.

By now it should be possible to understand the superiority of the proper text. Because of the time reference in "when", "Mine must walk when dead" can refer only to the state after death; thus the double perspective of the poem is lost. Likewise, "must" implies that Jane is to some extent controlled by a superior force; "would" indicates the dominance of her own will, whether in life or in death. The correct reading unravels what one critic has called "the tangle of tenses in the last stanza" and restores what another has called "one of Yeats's greatest triumphs" to its proper form.[12]

An examination of the proofs of *The Winding Stair and Other Poems*, then, can serve to heighten our admiration for the sureness of Yeats's hand. But these proofs have a further value: by studying them we can conclude that textual discrepancies between *The Winding Stair* and the *Collected Poems* are to be resolved in favour of the earlier collection. To reach such a conclusion is,

[12] Unterecker, p. 228; Parkinson, p. 215.

of course, to invite the charge of ignoring Yeats's final wishes. As we have seen, Yeats *did* have the opportunity to review the proofs of the *Collected Poems* after *The Winding Stair* had been published. But he had the proofs for no more than three days; and, having been assured that whatever corrections he made on the *Winding Stair* proofs would be incorporated into the *Collected Poems*, he is unlikely to have given much attention to the final section of the new volume.

More compelling than such speculation, however, are the differences between the two editions considered in light of *The Winding Stair* proofs. In citing these, I will give first the *Collected Poems* text and then *The Winding Stair* text.

A. "A Dialogue of Self and Soul", l. 65. "source,"/"source"
As noted above, Yeats wrote out the revised 11. 65–6 on the proof. As part of this revision he cancelled the comma.

B. "Blood and the Moon", l. 33. "pure,"/"pure:"
Thomas Mark changed the comma of the proofs to a semicolon. Yeats made no comment on the revision.

C. "Blood and the Moon", l. 45. "butterflies,"/"butterflies:" or "butterflies."
On the proofs the word was followed by a comma. Mark changed this to a period; this was printed as a colon in the English edition of *The Winding Stair* but correctly in the American text. Yeats did not remark the change.

D. "Coole and Ballylee, 1931", l. 34. "trees,"/"trees"
Yeats eliminated the comma.

E. "Byzantium", l. 19. "star-lit"/"starlit"
Yeats did not cancel Mark's note pointing out that "starlit" was the spelling used in l. 5 of the poem.

F. "The Mother of God", l. 1. "threefold"/"three-fold"
On the proofs Yeats changed "The three-fold terror of love; a fallen flare / Through the hollow of an ear;" to "Love's three-fold terror, a star's fallen flare / In the hollow of an ear;". But he then decided to revert to the original reading. The American edition of the *Collected Poems* retains the correct spelling, but the English text eliminates the hyphen.

G. "Vacillation", l. 30. "faith,"/"faith"
Yeats eliminated the comma.

H. "Crazy Jane on God", l. 5. "go;"/"go:"
The poem is not marked on the proofs.

I. "Crazy Jane Grown Old Looks at the Dancers", l. 6. "gleam;"/ "gleam:"
This part of the poem is not marked on the proofs.

J. "Crazy Jane Grown Old Looks at the Dancers", l. 12. "For no matter what is said"/"For, no matter what is said,"
Mark added the punctuation and Yeats let it stand.

K. "Crazy Jane Grown Old Looks at the Dancers", l. 13. "hate;"/"hate:"
This line is not marked on the proofs.

L. "Girl's Song", l. 7. "upright;"/"upright:"
Mark suggested that the comma of the proofs be changed to a colon and Yeats agreed.

M. "The Dancer at Cruachan and Cro-Patrick", l. 2. "men"/ "men,"
Yeats heavily revised the poem on the proofs, and in the process he accepted the comma which Mark had added at the end of l. 2, although he rejected the added comma at the end of l. 1.

N. "The Dancer at Cruachan and Cro-Patrick". [no note]/ [note]
On the proofs Mark provided a note: "Pronounce as if spelt 'Crockan' in modern Gaelic". Yeats revised this to "Pronounced in modern Gaelic as if spelt 'Crockan'". The *Collected Poems* does not offer the note.

O. "Tom the Lunatic", l. 13, "flood"/"flood,"
This part of the poem is not marked on the proofs. The proofs lack the comma, so Mark must have caught the error before going to press.

P. "Old Tom Again", l. 2. "swelling"/"yellow"
The poem is not marked on the proofs. As noted above, the misprint was corrected by an errata slip.

Q. "The Delphic Oracle Upon Poltinus", l. 1. "swim,"/"swim"
This part of the poem is not marked on the proofs.

R. "A First Confession", l. 4. "trembling,"/"trembling"
Mark eliminated the comma and Yeats made no comment.

In considering the above list, one should bear in mind that, first, there were numerous other revisions made on *The Winding Stair* proofs which were carried over into the *Collected Poems*; and, second, that Yeats had a great deal of confidence in Thomas Mark. Indeed, on 8 September 1932, Yeats asked Harold Macmillan to forward an enclosed letter to Mark, calling him "the admirable scholar who is assisting in the correction of proofs of my new collected edition": "It is partly a letter of thanks and partly an explanation of certain metrical tricks of mine which have puzzled him" (55003/136). As the present location of the letter to Mark is unknown, the passage quoted by Jon Stallworthy will have to suffice: "I have never been able to punctuate properly. I do not think I have ever differed from a correction of yours in punctuation. I suggest that in the remaining volumes you do not query your corrections."[13] Yeats was being overly modest − when he wanted to, which was often with his poems, he could be scrupulous (if idiosyncratic) with punctuation − and the "remaining volumes" did not of course include *Poems*; nevertheless, he was obviously impressed with Mark's abilities and with his dedication to the task.[14] Thus, when on *The Winding Stair* proofs Yeats failed to comment on a particular suggestion by Mark, it should not be assumed that he simply overlooked it.

Some of the differences between *The Winding Stair and Other*

[13] Jon Stallworthy, *Between the Lines: W. B. Yeats's Poetry in the Making* (Oxford: Clarendon Press, 1963), p. 12. In his reply, dated 12 September 1932, Mark said "It is very good of you to offer me a free hand with the punctuation. I was afraid of seeming fussy or pedantic, for one is always drawn on further than one expected in the attempt to make an edition of this kind harmonious in its smaller details" (*Letters to W. B. Yeats*, pp. 543−4).

[14] Most previous critics seem to me to have overstated Yeats's disdain for punctuation. Stallworthy, for example, quotes (p. 12) a letter from Yeats to Robert Bridges in which he wrote "I do not understand stops. I write my work so completely for the ear that I feel helpless when I have to measure pauses by stops & commas". But the text in question was an anthology printing, and to some extent Yeats was being deferential to the older poet. See *The Correspondence of Robert Bridges and W. B. Yeats*, ed. Richard J. Finneran (London: Macmillan, 1977), pp. 34−7, for the context of Yeats's remark.

On the other hand, Curtis Bradford was a staunch defender of Yeats's punctuation, both in his review of the *Variorum Poems* in *Sewanee Review*, 68, No. 4 (Autumn 1958), 668−78, esp. 673−4, and in his *Yeats at Work* (Carbondale and Edwardsville: Southern Illinois University Press, 1965), pp. 13−14. Bradford concluded that "the long line of editors and copy readers who added punctuation to Yeats's own versions of his poems have done us no favor" (*Yeats at Work*, p. 393, n. 1).

Poems and the *Collected Poems* are obviously unremarkable, and
it would be difficult to make a case on either side. However, it
seems to me that although there is *never* an instance where the
Collected Poems is clearly superior, in the case of a substantial
number of the discrepancies *The Winding Stair* must be considered the better text. We might consider, for instance, ll. 43–6
of "Blood and the Moon".

> Upon the dusty, glittering windows cling,
> And seem to cling upon the moonlit skies,
> Tortoiseshell butterflies, peacock butterflies.
> A couple of night-moths are on the wing.

Read aloud, the passage demands the full stop. The significance of
the passage is found in the *contrast* between the butterflies and the
night-moths, a contrast heightened by diction and rhythm.
Butterflies to Yeats are of course a "fabulous symbol", suggesting
"the crooked road of intuition" and "wisdom" as well as the soul
(*The Hour-Glass*). In "Blood and the Moon" the butterflies are
elaborate and beautiful, but Yeats recognises that they are
essentially fictive, unreal: they look like peacocks, they appear to
be made of tortoiseshell.[15] "Their ascent aborted by imprisonment
within the tower", as Daniel A. Harris has suggested, they "seem to
cling" upon windows that are "glittering" but also "dusty".[16] Thus
the butterflies hearken back to an earlier age ("In mockery I have
set / A powerful emblem up"), an age in which "Shelley had his
towers, thought's crowned powers he called them once". In the
modern world, the butterflies have been superseded by "a couple
of night-moths". The point about the night-moths is precisely that
they have no symbolic value: night-moths are, well, night-moths.
Here they are "on the wing": not trying to ascend the tower or even
to escape from it, but moving relentlessly towards their own

[15] As David R. Clark has suggested to me, Yeats — with his early training as a
naturalist — would have of course been aware of the existence of the peacock
butterfly ("a European butterfly [*Vanessa Io*] with ocellated wings") and the
tortoise-shell butterfly ("one of several butterflies, esp. the European *Vanessa
urticae* and *V. polychlorous*, and the American *Aglais milberti*"), to give the
OED definitions. However, it seems to me that in the poem what is important is
not the lepidopteral accuracy but the metamorphic adjectives.

[16] Daniel A. Harris, *Yeats: Coole Park & Ballylee* (Baltimore and London: Johns
Hopkins University Press, 1974), p. 220. Harris's suggestive reading of "Blood
and the Moon" is found on pp. 213–22.

destruction. It is thus the contrast between the butterflies and the night-moths, between the fabulous and the mundane, that leads Yeats to offer in the next lines his summary speculation/judgment on his own age: "Is every modern nation like the tower, / Half dead at the top?"

In sum, then, the available evidence strongly suggests that the differences between *The Winding Stair and Other Poems* and the *Collected Poems* are not the result of Yeats's last-minute revisions on the proofs for the later volume but of the publisher's failure properly to collate the two editions, first when Yeats returned both sets of proofs together and later when *The Winding Stair* was in print and the *Collected Poems* still in proof.[17] I have therefore used *The Winding Stair* final page proofs as the basic text for that section of the new *Poems*.

The only other instance in which the text of the 1933 *Collected Poems* has not been followed concerns "The Phases of the Moon" and "All Souls' Night". Here it is evident that Yeats made significant revisions in both poems for the second edition of *A Vision* in 1937, and those later versions have been preferred for the new *Poems*.

With those exceptions, however, the first English edition of the *Collected Poems* offers the most reliable basic text for those poems included. We have already outlined how that collection came to have its two sections of "Lyrical" and "Narrative and Dramatic". But Yeats introduced into the *Collected Poems* one other massive change from the Edition de Luxe *Poems*. On the final page proofs for the earlier volume (dated 3 August 1932), the middle part of *The Tower* section contained the following lyrics:

> "Two Songs from a Play"
> "Wisdom"
> "Leda and the Swan"
> "On a Picture of a Black Centaur by Edmund Dulac"
> "Among School Children"
> "Colonus' Praise"
> "The Hero, the Girl, and the Fool"

---

[17] Thomas Mark would obviously have been under pressure from his superiors to get *The Winding Stair and Other Poems* into print as quickly as possible, so that a decent interval could pass between it and the *Collected Poems* and so that the *Collected Poems* could still be available for the Christmas season. Macmillan, New York, did not follow such a plan and therefore was able to publish the *Collected Poems* two weeks in advance of the English edition.

In the process of reading the proofs of the *Collected Poems*, Yeats must have made two related decisions. First, he would eliminate the first seventeen lines of "The Hero, the Girl, and the Fool", allowing the last ten lines to remain under the title "The Fool by the Roadside". Second, he would add to the collection a new poem entitled "Fragments", consisting of a four-line poem from the Introduction to *The Words upon the Window Pane*, published in the *Dublin Magazine* for October–December 1931, and a six-line poem from the Introduction to *The Resurrection*, then unpublished but later to be included in *Wheels and Butterflies*. I am in fact uncertain about which decision was made first, but I offer the above order as more probable because Yeats had always been uneasy about "The Hero, the Girl, and the Fool": it was published in both the 1922 *Seven Poems and a Fragment* (under the title "Cuchulain the Girl and the Fool") and the 1928 *The Tower*; but in the 1925 *A Vision* only "The Fool by the Roadside" was included. I am more sure that the changes were made during the second and final correction of the *Collected Poems* proofs from 27–30 September 1933, as in their letter acknowledging receipt of the corrected proofs, the publishers assured Yeats that "we will see that the necessary alterations are made to the Contents list" (55744/541).

Once Yeats had decided on these changes, he also took the opportunity to modify the order of the poems. In the *Collected Poems* we have the following:

"Two Songs from a Play"
"Fragments"
"Leda and the Swan"
"On a Picture of a Black Centaur by Edmund Dulac"
"Among School Children"
"Colonus' Praise"
"Wisdom"
"The Fool by the Roadside"

Some time after Yeats's death (I think in the spring of 1939), it was discovered that "Fragments" was not included on the Edition de Luxe proofs. The solution to this problem was an instruction by Thomas Mark to add "Fragments" before "Wisdom" while leaving everything else unchanged. Thus when *Poems* (1949) used the Edition de Luxe proofs as its basic text, we are presented with *both* a contents and an ordering never approved by Yeats:

"Two Songs from a Play"
"Fragments"
"Wisdom"
"Leda and the Swan"
"On a Picture of a Black Centaur by Edmund Dulac"
"Among School Children"
"Colonus' Praise"
"The Hero, the Girl, and the Fool"[18]

As there is no evidence supporting the arrangement in the 1949 *Poems*, there is no need to argue here the clear superiority of the *Collected Poems* format; and to do so properly would involve a detailed analysis of the structure of *The Tower*. Instead, we must abandon strict chronology and, delaying our discussion of the later volumes in Yeats's canon, expand on the posthumous history of his texts.

[18] When in 1956 the eighth printing of the American *Collected Poems* was supposedly brought into conformity with *Poems* (1949), "The Fool by the Roadside" was replaced by "The Hero, the Girl, and the Fool", but the order of the poems was left unchanged from the 1933 collection. Thus we have yet *another* contents and ordering not approved by Yeats.

CHAPTER THREE

Collaborative Revision: Thomas Mark and George Yeats, 1939–49

Yeats died on 28 January 1939. He had not been long in his temporary resting-place at Roquebrune before the process began of — not to put too fine a point on it — corrupting the texts which he had worked so hard to perfect. The defects in *Poems* (1949) which we have so far noted can essentially be traced to the original fatal decision to prefer the proofs of the Edition de Luxe over the *Collected Poems*. But we now enter a realm where even the best of intentions were sometimes compromised and where, sadly, Yeats's own judgment was occasionally disregarded. In this chapter I shall describe that process in a general way and illustrate it principally by its effect on the *Collected Poems*, reserving its consequences for the post-1933 collections until we take up those volumes in turn.

At the time of Yeats's death there had been very little recent activity on the Edition de Luxe (hereafter to be referred to as the Coole Edition). Macmillan was obviously not anxious to undertake the project amid the changing economic conditions of the period, and the supposedly forthcoming Scribner Edition provided further motivation for delay. Yeats had first described the Scribner Edition in a letter to Macmillan on 18 November 1935, explaining that he had received a letter from George P. Brett, Jr., propos-ing that Macmillan, New York, "in combination with Charles Scribners' Sons should bring out a subscription set of my work in seven or eight volumes, 70 or 80 dollars a set, limiting the edition to, at the utmost, 750 sets[,] not to be on 'sale at the bookstores. It would be sold solely by mail order and house to house canvas'" (55003/193). Yeats estimated his potential earnings at $2500–4800. The London publishers were less than delighted with this peculiarly American proposal — Yeats's works somehow equated with vacuum cleaners — but they were in no position to object. On 27 November 1935, Harold Macmillan told Yeats's agent that "since, however, we have, quite frankly, felt difficulty in pursuing our edition with any vigour, in the present state of the market, I am very glad that this American proposal has come along, which will give Mr. Yeats a substantial profit and will not impede the publication of an English edition" (55774/153). A year later, on 14 November 1936, Macmillan told Watt that "it would be judicious for us to hold over our edition for the time being" but still refused "to let Scribners have the sheets or corrected proofs of our own edition," explaining "that the more divergence there could be between our edition and Scribners, the better it would be in the interests of the former" (55787/444—5). Over the next two years there were periodic inquiries of Yeats as to how his new works should be fitted into the collected edition, but no serious thought was given to actual publication.

Yeats's death, however, produced a flurry of activity on the Coole Edition: now it could be, at least in theory, a "complete" edition; and the publicity associated with his death would not be a detriment to sales. Correspondence between Macmillan and Mrs Yeats about the Coole Edition was exchanged as early as 8 February 1939 (55819/189—90). On 21 February 1939, Mrs Yeats explained that she would be in London for the Memorial Service at St Martin-in-the-Fields in March and suggested a meeting.[1] On 28 February 1939 Harold Macmillan sent Mrs Yeats a lengthy letter about the Coole Edition and requested "the text of any further poems which ought to go into the edition" (55820/204).

Mrs Yeats met with the publishers in London on 17 March 1939. Among the issues discussed was the possibility of adding a further volume to the Coole Edition, to include, as she wrote on 13 April 1939, "some autobiographical material in MSS, and also some uncollected essays". Finally, on 17 April 1939 Mrs Yeats sent Mark typescripts of *New Poems* and *Last Poems*. After commenting on that material, she also noted that

> there are two small corrections in the Collected Poems, written into his copy of book. Page 197, 6 lines from bottom of page, 'Athen*e*' not 'Athen*a*'. Page 422, last line, 'wandering' instead of 'whirling'. These two corrections were made for sound. Have you got them in your edition de Luxe?

[1] Unless otherwise indicated, letters not followed by a British Library manuscript number are found in the Archives of Macmillan, London, in Basingstoke.

The references here are to "Michael Robartes and the Dancer" (l. 19) and "The Two Kings" (l. 183). But strictly speaking, Mrs Yeats's letter is not correct, as Yeats's own copy of the *Collected Poems* includes only the latter change. However, in the copy of the volume inscribed "Michael Yeats from W B Yeats November 1933", Yeats did make both revisions, also changing "Athena" to "Athene" in "The Phases of the Moon" (l. 45). On the other hand, for the 1937 edition of *A Vision*, Yeats used "Athena" in a revised version of "The Phases of the Moon". More importantly, on the final page proofs for the Cuala Press *New Poems*, marked by Yeats "Press", he changed "Athene" to "Athena" in "Beautiful Lofty Things". The Cuala Press failed to make the correction. Nevertheless, in the new *Poems* I have followed what appears to be his last known wish (as well as the standard spelling) and have used "Athena" throughout. The revision in "The Two Kings" of "whirling" to "wandering" has of course been adopted. Michael B. Yeats's copy of the *Collected Poems* contains two further changes by Yeats: "Guare" to "Guaire" in "The Three Beggars" (ll. 8, 19, 26, 54) and "Early" to "Earley" in the "[Introductory Lines]" to *The Shadowy Waters*. Only the first of those emendations has been admitted into the new edition of *Poems*.[2]

In her letter Mrs Yeats went on to ask

When you have made your own list of corrections to the completed volume of *Poems* would you send me the complete proofs? You see I am left 'literary executor'. WBY wrote to you in September (or October) 1932 about punctuation and generally asking your help, without which he could never get his work

---

[2] This copy of the 1933 *Collected Poems* is in the collection of Michael B. Yeats. Unless otherwise indicated, all other annotated copies of Yeats's works are in the collection of Miss Anne Yeats.

It is true that the spelling "Earley" appears in both the 1935 Cuala Press and the 1936 Macmillan editions of *Dramatis Personae* (pp. 20/19), though the first text may be misprinted and the second descends from the first. However, Yeats used "Early" in all published editions of the poem as well as in some early articles, especially "Ireland Bewitched" in *The Contemporary Review* for September 1899 (see *Uncollected Prose by W. B. Yeats*, II, ed. John P. Frayne and Colton Johnson [London: Macmillan, 1975], esp. 171–83). "Early" is also the spelling in Yeats's primary source, Lady Gregory; and it is, of course, a proper name. I have thus decided against accepting Yeats's slip.

The correction to "Earley" is in fact cancelled in pencil; but I believe that cancellation was done by Mrs Yeats at the same time that she added other pencil markings to her son's copy of the *Collected Poems*.

into the final form he wished. There are, however, a few metrical 'tricks' as he called them, and tricks of repetition of words and phrases, deliberately used, which we should, I think, carefully preserve.

In his response on 21 April 1939, Mark promised to make the alterations in the *Collected Poems* and assured her of "proofs of both volumes of poems, with any queries I may have to raise, before they go to the printers for press", adding "I shall feel much more satisfied if I can refer matters of this kind to you" (55882/550, 552).

On 2 June 1939, Harold Macmillan inquired from Mrs Yeats when she would be able to receive "the complete marked proofs of the two volumes of *Poems*", now grown from the single volume in the Edition de Luxe, and "when you think you might be able to return them finally for press" (55824/586−9). The proofs were forwarded to her on 8 June 1939 (55825/171). On 12 June 1939, Mrs Yeats returned the proofs of the first volume, accompanied by a list of fifteen proper names that were misspelled, mainly of figures in Irish mythology. As it is at least possible that Yeats's spelling is a key to his pronunciation and thus to the sound of his poetry, and since Gaelic spelling is itself not fully codified, I have not accepted these suggested changes in the *Complete Poems*.[3] Mark, however, incorporated all but one of them into *Poems*.[4] Moreover, Mrs Yeats's comment on "The Fiddler of Dooney" − "I suggest a note to explain the pronunciation of Mocharabuiee, as I often hear it mispronounced when the poem is being broadbast etc. '*Pronounced as if spelt* "*Mockrabwee*'" − resulted in an added note in *Poems*. Unattributed, it has been incorrectly assumed to be by Yeats (as in *VP* 178).

On 14 June 1939, Mrs Yeats returned the second volume of the Coole Edition *Poems*, along with a list of suggested changes. Of those that concern us here, three were the correction of apparent misprints. She also corrected "Shaw Taylor" of "Coole Park, 1929"

[3] For instance, Mrs Yeats corrected Yeats's "Coloony" to "Colooney", whereas the standard spelling, according to James P. McGarry's *Place Names in the Writings of W. B. Yeats*, ed. Edward Malins (Gerrards Cross, Bucks.: Colin Smythe, 1976), p. 33, is "Collooney".

[4] Mrs Yeats incorrectly changed the title of Standish Hayes O'Grady's *Silva Gadelica* to *Silva Gaedelica*, but the error was caught by someone before *Poems* was published. I suspect she was repeating the mistake of Lady Gregory in the Notes to *Gods and Fighting Men*.

(l. 14) to "Shawe-Taylor"; as there is of course no question of spelling variation in this instance, and since Yeats had previously spelled the name correctly in both verse and prose, this change has been adopted in the new *Poems*. A fifth revision, the addition of a hyphen after "and" in "haystack- and roof-levelling wind" in "A Prayer for my Daughter" (l. 5), was not accepted by Mark. But the most interesting exchange between Mrs Yeats and Mark concerns "Coole and Ballylee, 1931".

Since the proofs for the two-volume Coole Edition *Poems* (which unfortunately do not survive) were printed from the 1932 Edition de Luxe *Poems*, "Coole and Ballylee, 1931" was in the seven-stanza form found in the 1929 Fountain Press edition of *The Winding Stair*. On the proofs of the 1933 *The Winding Stair and Other Poems*, Yeats had removed the sixth stanza and published it separately as "The Choice", changing one punctuation mark and revising "And when the story's finished" to "When all that story's finished" (l. 5). Yeats also agreed to Mark's suggestion that the title be shortened from "Coole Park and Ballylee, 1931", "to avoid having &" in the running titles. What caught Mrs Yeats's eye was the different wording of the fifth line. She asked Mark, "did WBY alter this in earlier proof? Cf. Collected Poems p. 279 ["The Choice"]". To resolve this discrepancy, Mark went back and checked the 1932 proofs. He then told Mrs Yeats that "I find that, when this edition was first in proof, before the Collected Poems appeared, *The Choice* was verse VI of 'Coole Park and Ballylee'. 'When all that story's finished' is evidently, as you pointed out, the later text. Thank you". Mrs Yeats's response is surprising: "I should be inclined to keep the *two* versions, using later version for The Choice only??"

This very interesting episode illustrates the aura of reverence surrounding the Edition de Luxe *Poems*, at least in the minds of George Yeats and Thomas Mark. Mrs Yeats was willing to disregard Yeats's revision and publish "Coole Park and Ballylee, 1931" in the seven-stanza form. Mark was not willing to go to that extreme; but even though he wrote on the 1932 proof that "The Collected Poems text must be the later and correct one", he did not apply that principle to the title, which reverts to the longer form in *Poems* (1949). And, so far as I can discover, it never occurred to either of them that the two-part division of the *Collected Poems* into "Lyrical" and "Narrative and Dramatic" was likewise "later and correct".

In any event, Mark acknowledged receipt of the proofs for the two-volume *Poems* on 16 June 1939, telling Mrs Yeats that her corrections "will be very helpful" (55825/452). Harold Macmillan had written her in a similar vein on 13 June 1939: "Mr. Mark has told me of the very kind help you are giving him with the proofs, and I am pleased that you have been able to collaborate so actively with the edition" (55825/302–3). Mark must have sent Mrs Yeats some more notes in the next few days, as she wrote to him on 22 June 1939, suggesting that "the Gaelic spellings should be altered where necessary owing to WBY's note at the end of POEMS ["The Spelling of Gaelic Names", VP 840]. As you know, his spelling of quite simple English words was very uncertain." She added that she had overlooked the spelling of "Guaire" in "The Three Beggars" until she had been reading the Coole Edition *Plays* (King Guaire is a character in *The King's Threshold*) but had now "verified the spelling at the National Library". But of more interest are Mark's notes and her comments on them, particularly the two notes about the poems.

Mark had first asked, "If Ulad should be Uladh, ought Aed, in *The Wanderings of Oisin*, to be Aedh?" Her answer was a straightforward "yes". "Aed" occurs but once in the poem (Book II, l. 87), in a passage added in the 1895 *Poems*. In other poems, Yeats spelled the name "Aodh" (in 1898) and "Aedh" (in 1899). However, as Yeats had innumerable opportunities to modify "Aed" and did not do so, and since "AEd" is the spelling in his primary source (Standish O'Grady's *History of Ireland* [1878–80]), I have not accepted Mrs Yeats's revision in the new *Poems*. Mark's other comment concerned "The Song of Wandering Aengus":

Lines 1 and 3 of verse 2 both end with 'on the floor'. Miss Hartnoll, of our staff, once spoke to Mr Yeats about this, and he said he thought he had intended line 3 to end with 'by the door'. We had no note of this, however, and the change would have to be authorised.

The implication is clearly that Mrs Yeats's "authority" would suffice. Luckily, she was conservative in this instance, though not without some debate:

I several times heard him end line 3 as 'by the door', but on one occasion (at a lecture) he stopped & said "No: I must start

again", & then said the line "on the floor". So I think perhaps
leave it as printed?

Had the change been admitted, Yeats's careful use of a major
repetition in each stanza ("hazel," "floor," "lands") to foreshadow
the hypnotic "And . . . and . . . / And . . . / And" of lines 20–2
would have been lost.

On 30 June 1939 Mark sent Mrs Yeats "one or two afterthoughts
about the poems for your consideration" (55826/175); these were
returned to him on 5 July 1939. Of those that concern us here, one
was a query about the proper spelling of "MacGregor" in "All
Souls' Night", but the other was more interesting:

> 'Tom O'Roughley' in *The Wild Swans* verse 2, line 5. 'trumpeter
> Michael'. I queried this in a prose book, I think. The trumpeter
> is usually Gabriel, and I have not found any suitable legend
> about Michael. Do you think it should be 'trumpeter Gabriel'?[5]

Mrs Yeats was likewise uncertain, but another reference in Yeats's
poems was able to preserve the correct reading:

> I also agree about no legend about trumpeter Michael, but in
> "The Happy Townland" we have "Michael will unhook his
> trumpet" & so I think we might leave Michael as trumpeter?

Work on other Yeats volumes continued through the autumn of
1939. Despite the suspension of the Coole Edition because of the

---

[5] Mark is recalling a reference in "J. M. Synge and the Ireland of his Time" to
"Saint Michael with the trumpet that calls the body to resurrection". *Essays and
Introductions* (London: Macmillan, 1961), p. 316.

   In *William Butler Yeats and the Irish Literary Revival* (New York: McClure,
Phillips, 1904), p. 106, Horatio Sheafe Krans had complained of the "wanton
obscurity" of the fifth stanza of "The Happy Townland". A response was
offered by Patty Gurd in *The Early Poetry of William Butler Yeats* (Lancaster,
Pennsylvania: New Era Printing Company, 1916), p. 82: "Stanza 4 [sic] has
puzzled the critics, for so far they have attempted to explain it by mystic ideas. I
take it, that the contents of this quaint and charming stanza are the gleanings of
a walk through the Dublin Art Museum, of expeditions into the country, and of
archeological knowledge gained, perhaps, from books. 'Michael unhooking his
trumpet from a bough overhead' [sic] is a reminiscence of Celtic mythology, of
Geraint, perhaps, or some other hero of the Arthurian cycle." One would give
much to know Yeats's response to both critics. I owe the references to George
Brandon Saul, *Prolegomena to the Study of Yeats's Poems* (Philadelphia:
University of Pennsylvania Press, 1957), p. 82.

war, Mark was anxious to complete the proofreading. Mrs Yeats, however, appears to have lost interest in the project, and on 12 February 1940 Mark complained to Watt that "I have written to her several times about some outstanding proofs of the big edition of her husband's works, but have had no reply" (55834/523). Many years later, on 12 May 1949, Harold Macmillan would remind A. P. Watt "how difficult we found it to get a reply from her".

Probably in March 1949, however, Mark must have written Mrs Yeats to inquire if line 39 of "The Song of the Happy Shepherd" should read "Rewording" or "Rewarding" "in melodious guile." She responded as follows:

> You are right about "Rewording in melodious guile". This was printed until the 1912 Fisher Unwin edition of *Poems*, in that volume the spelling was changed to 'rewarding'. (obviously a printer's error for the 1912 edition is in different type & there is [sic] no other changes in the poems.)

This is in fact incorrect: the change first appears in the 1904 edition of *Poems*. The 1906 *Poetical Works* and the 1908 *Collected Works*, which I suspect may both descend from the 1901 *Poems*, revert to "Rewording"; but all other editions published in Yeats's lifetime use "Rewarding".[6] Mark of course took Mrs Yeats's suggestion, and the 1949 *Poems* reads "Rewording".

To decide on the better reading in the light of the available evidence is to deal in probabilities. Of the fifty or so differences between the 1901 and 1904 texts of *Poems*, some are corrections of obvious misprints while others introduce new misprints. All but one of the remaining revisions are improvements of the kind that it might be possible to assign to a zealous copy-editor. Other than "Rewording"/"Rewarding", the only change which seems certainly beyond any copy-editor is the revision in spelling of "Cuhoolin" to "Cuchulain". Like "Rewarding" and some of the other minor revisions, that change carries over into the latter printings.

[6] For another example of Yeats forgetting to submit the latest revised text as copy for a new edition, see "*The Tables of the Law*: A Critical Text", ed. Robert O'Driscoll, *Yeats Studies*, 1 (Bealtaine, 1971), 87–118. Yeats would have recalled that the 1901 *Poems* included a new revised version of *The Countess Cathleen*, and he might well have forgotten about the relatively minor changes in the 1904 *Poems*.

The page proofs for the 1906 volume of *The Poetical Works* are in the Berg Collection of the New York Public Library. "Rewording" is not marked.

Those readers who prefer "Rewording" will agree with Mrs Yeats that "Rewarding" was simply a misprint which Yeats failed to catch. Those who prefer "Rewarding" will suggest that it is difficult to believe that Yeats would have missed the "error" in the eleven further editions of *Poems*; in the 1925 *Early Poems and Stories*, for which he went through his work with some care; and especially in the 1933 *Collected Poems*, where for the first time "The Song of the Happy Shepherd" is placed at the very threshold of his poetic canon. Such a reader might also argue that the revision eliminates the awkward if not illogical reference to "Rewording . . . / Thy fretful words". I find the latter position persuasive, and in the new *Poems* I have left stand "Rewarding".

In her letter to Mark, Mrs Yeats also asked about the fate of the two-volume *Poems*. Mark was able to reply that "the limited two-volume edition of the Poems has waited a long time, but we are announcing it for this autumn". The remainder of their 1949 correspondence concentrates on the text of *Last Poems*, and we shall come to that in a later chapter.

From what has been said so far, one might conclude that the 1933 *Collected Poems* was subjected to very little posthumous revision. But we have yet to consider the changes introduced in the 1949 *Poems* without any discussion by Mark and Mrs Yeats in their surviving correspondence. First, excluding *The Winding Stair and Other Poems* section (for reasons explained in Chapter 2), there are over twenty variants between the 1932 final proofs of the Edition de Luxe *Poems* and the *Collected Poems*. There are two possible explanations for these differences: (1) they represent revisions which Yeats (or Mark) made on the proofs of the *Collected Poems*; (2) they represent errors introduced in the printing of the *Collected Poems* which Yeats and Mark failed to catch while the book was in production (and, for those not marked in his personal copy, which Yeats also failed to notice before his death and which were not called to his attention by Mrs Yeats or other dedicated readers of his verse). To decide on the proper explanation for any particular variant, given the lack of any surviving proofs for the *Collected Poems*, is often difficult − if not indeed impossible from a strictly textual analysis. However, the decision to prefer the Edition de Luxe proofs over the *Collected Poems* of course means that the 1949 *Poems* consistently uses the 1932 readings in these instances (except for "Athena"/"Athene" and "Guare"/"Guaire").

As we shall see, with some exceptions this choice results in a corrupt text.

But Mark was not content simply to reproduce the 1932 proofs. He also introduced over seventy-five changes in the 1933 *Collected Poems* as printed in the two-volume *Poems*.[7] Writing to Mark on 14 June 1939, Mrs Yeats told him "I return the second vol of POEMS with one or two suggestions. With two exceptions all your corrections are left". Again, although a very few of these revisions seem required, most of them are not. A few examples of the several kinds of errors in the 1949 *Poems* will have to suffice.

A. "The Fascination of What's Difficult", l. 8.

All editions in Yeats's lifetime as well as the 1932 proofs read "road metal". Mark, who was much fonder of the hyphen than was Yeats, changed this to "road-metal". This revision may strike most readers as trivial in the extreme. But what of l. 61 of "Among School Children", where one has a choice between Mark's "O chestnut-tree, great-rooted blossomer" and Yeats's "O chestnut tree, great rooted blossomer"?

B. "[Introductory Rhymes]", l. 3.

The 1932 proofs, following the earlier printings, read "free of ten and four". For the *Collected Poems* Yeats revised this to "free of the ten and four", but the 1949 *Poems* reverts to the earlier reading. However, as early as 1916 the phrase was revised to "free of the ten and four" in Yeats's note to the poem; and Yeats, who further revised the note in 1933, or Mark must have caught the discrepancy (see VP 817–8).

C. "The Tower", l. 193.

All editions in Yeats's lifetime as well as the 1932 proofs punctuate as below the brilliant conclusion of the poem, in which the speaker vows to "study / In a learned school" until "what worse evil come—"

> The death of friends, or death
> Of every brilliant eye

[7] This approximate figure does not include the poems from *The Winding Stair and Other Poems* section of the *Collected Poems*. For the reasons noted in the previous chapter, by following the 1932 proofs in *Poems* (1949), Mark introduced numerous misreadings into that section. To cite just one example, in the posthumous edition l. 39 of "Coole and Ballylee, 1931" reads "We shift about" instead of the revised version, "Man shifts about".

> That made a catch in the breath—
> Seem but the clouds of the sky
> When the horizon fades;
> Or a bird's sleepy cry
> Among the deepening shades.

Mark's "correction" of the semi-colon after "fades" to a comma does incalculable harm not only to the rhythm of the passage but also to the contrast in scope and significance between "the clouds of the sky" and "a bird's sleepy cry".

D. "The Two Kings", l. 189.
All editions in Yeats's lifetime as well as the 1932 proofs print the relevant passage as follows:

> "How should I love," I answered,
> "Were it not that when the dawn has lit my bed
> And shown my husband sleeping there, I have sighed,
> 'Your strength and nobleness will pass away.'

Mark altered the period to a question mark, which changes the sense of the passage and also eliminates the contrast with the following three lines, which Yeats *does* phrase in the interrogative:

> Or how should love be worth its pains were it not
> That when he has fallen asleep within my arms,
> Being wearied out, I love in man the child?

The last two examples are more complex.

E. "The Withering of the Boughs", l. 13.
The 1932 proofs, following the earlier printings, read:

> I know where a dim moon drifts, where the Danaan kind
> Wind and unwind their dances when the light grows cool
> On the island lawns, their feet where the pale foam gleams.

In the *Collected Poems*, this was revised to "Wind and unwind dancing when the light grows cool". This is possibly a printer's error, but a close examination of the spacing of l. 13 in the first edition of the *Collected Poems* suggests otherwise. Had the compositor misread the line and started out to set "Wind and unwind dancing when the light grows cool", which contains forty-nine characters and spaces, there would have been no need to indent "cool" on the line below. Indeed, in l. 19 he was able to squeeze fifty-three characters and spaces into one line without indentation; and, other than l. 13, the shortest line in the poem to be indented also has fifty-three characters and spaces (l. 12). Moreover, the amount of spacing between the first five words of "Wind and unwind dancing when the light grows cool" strongly suggests that the compositor was attempting to replace "their dances" with "dancing" without having to change the indented position of "cool".

F. "Solomon to Sheba", l. 17.

All earlier printings as well as the 1932 proofs read "Sang Solomon to Sheba", which parallels the opening of the other two stanzas ("Sang Solomon to Sheba"; "To Solomon sang Sheba"). In the *Collected Poems* the line appears as "Said Solomon to Sheba". This is obviously a likely candidate for a printer's error. However, it is also possible that Yeats made the revision on the *Collected Poems* proofs, in which case "Said" would signify Solomon's desire to terminate the conversation and to turn to other activities. Short of the discovery of the proofs of the *Collected Poems*, "Said"/"Sang" is likely to remain a textual crux in Yeats's poetry. In the new *Poems* I have offered "Said", in the hope that Yeats or Mark (or, perhaps especially in this case, Mrs Yeats) would have noticed the error if it was one.

If, as I believe, Thomas Mark was wrong in the above instances as well as in many not cited, he was not always so. I have followed him, for example, in extending Yeats's note on the pronunciation of "Cruachan", written for "The Dancer at Cruachan and Cro-Patrick" in *The Winding Stair and Other Poems* and attached to "The Hour before Dawn" in the *Collected Poems*, to "The Old Age of Queen Maeve", as was done for the 1949 *Poems*. The remaining emendations in the new *Poems* to works which appeared in the 1933 *Collected Poems* are as follows:

A. "The Indian to His Love", ll. 15–16.

In the *Collected Poems*, the last two stanzas are printed as one. On the 1932 proofs, the third stanza ended at the bottom of a page.

B. "In the Seven Woods", l. 14.

"Parc-na-lee", the reading of both the 1932 proofs and the *Collected Poems* (earlier printings had "Parc-na-Lee") has been revised to "Pairc-na-lee". Yeats made this correction himself on the 1932 proofs in l. 7 of ["I walked among the seven woods of Coole"].

C. "Broken Dreams", l. 36.

"For old sakes' sake", the reading of all editions in Yeats's lifetime, has been corrected to "For old sake's sake". The correction was in fact made on the 1932 proofs, but possibly not by Yeats.

D. "The Wanderings of Oisin", Book III, l. 169.

All earlier printings as well as the 1932 proofs read "And because I went by them so huge and so speedy with eyes so bright, / Came after the hard gaze of youth, or an old man lifted his head". In the *Collected Poems*, this becomes "And before I went by them". It is remotely possible that Yeats made the change on the proofs of the *Collected Poems*, but with the revision the passage seems senseless.

Most of the textual problems we have so far discussed involve poems with a long textual history — in some cases, one stretching over five decades. We now turn to the works published in the last five years of Yeats's life, where two printings is the usual maximum and some poems were never seen through the press. The textual problems therefore become, if anything, more crucial.

CHAPTER FOUR

A Full Moon in March and *New Poems*

After the 1933 *Collected Poems*, Yeats did not issue any new poetry in book form in London until *A Full Moon in March*, published on 22 November 1935 in an edition of 2000 copies. This contained only a relatively few poems, gathered under the heading "Parnell's Funeral and Other Poems". Yeats described the volume to Ethel Mannin as "Not much in it − illness interfered" (L 844), overlooking the numerous other projects he had been engaged on during 1934−35.

Most of the poems in the volume had already appeared in *The King of the Great Clock Tower, Commentaries and Poems*, published by the Cuala Press on 14 December 1934 and by Macmillan, New York, in May 1935. Yeats seems to have made no attempt to have this volume published by Macmillan, London, probably wanting to protect the sales of the Cuala printing. But early in June 1935 Yeats must have instructed his agent to send his English publishers the materials for a new volume. Macmillan replied to Watt on 13 June 1935 as follows:

> Many thanks for your letter of June 7th enclosing 'copy' for Mr. Yeats's new work entitled 'The King of the Great Clock Tower', or rather, as he now intends to call it, 'A Full Moon in March'. We shall, of course, be glad to publish this, but I suggest we had better wait for actual publication until the Autumn. (55768/147)

On 9 September 1935, Macmillan was able to forward "a marked set of the page proofs of 'A Full Moon in March', together with the original typescript" (55771/152). Yeats returned the proofs within a few days: on 16 September 1935 Macmillan acknowledged receipt and said "your corrections are quite clear, and a revise will reach you shortly" (55771/319). The final proofs were sent to

Yeats on 26 September 1935; he must have had them but a single day, as they were back with the publishers, passed for press, two days later (55771/554, 589). On 1 October 1935 Macmillan received a correction to the text of *The King of the Great Clock Tower* and replied that they could "make the alteration without any difficulty" (55771/626). Two weeks later, though, they were forced to inform Yeats that the production of the volume was "too far advanced" to allow for the insertion of some music to accompany *The King of the Great Clock Tower*. Interestingly, the publishers suggested "that it might be well to reserve it, with your approval, as one of the special features of the big collected edition of your works, which we still have in hand. I take it that anything new we have published for you is to be added to the material for that edition" (55772/332).

Although *A Full Moon in March* may have presented no particular problems to Yeats and his publishers, the same cannot be said of the treatment of the poetry from the volume in the new *Poems*. The first problem concerns the very title of the section itself. The heading used in the 1949 *Poems* is "From 'A Full Moon in March'". Since I know of no evidence that Yeats had thought of or approved such an awkward title, I have replaced it by his own "Parnell's Funeral and Other Poems", a title which occupies a full page in the 1935 collection. A second and more important problem is the inclusion in *Poems* (1949) of "Three Songs to the Same Tune", which of course also appears in a revised form as "Three Marching Songs" in *Last Poems*. The printing of both versions was the decision of Mrs Yeats. She wrote to Mark on 17 April 1939 as follows:

> You will see that he re-wrote (for about the ninth time) the "Three Marching Songs" which were published in "A Full Moon in March". I have discussed with various poets the question as to whether the *final versions only* should be published, and there seems to be unanimous agreement that *both* versions should be printed, as they are, on the whole, so different.

The "various poets" would almost surely have included F. R. Higgins and Frank O'Connor.

Mrs Yeats is using here the same logic as we saw in the previous chapter in her suggestion that both the seven-stanza "Coole and Ballylee, 1931" and "The Choice" might be included in *Poems*.

Although Mark did not accept that suggestion, with "Three Marching Songs" he offered no protest against the "unanimous agreement" of Mrs Yeats and her advisers. It seems clear, however, that Yeats intended the revised version to *replace* "Three Songs to the Same Tune" and that he would not have wanted both texts to remain in his standard canon. Not only had that been his usual practice since the beginning of his career — even in the face of attacks from several critics that his revisions were ruining his poems and that the old versions were superior — but in this particular instance Yeats took his own copy of *A Full Moon in March* and began the process of revision (in ink) directly on the text of the poem. This is a certain indication that in Yeats's mind "Three Songs to the Same Tune" was to be superseded. He changed the title to "Three Revolutionary Songs" and drafted a note reading "I published a first confused version of these songs some years ago. I hope they are now clear & perhaps singable". I have therefore not included "Three Songs to the Same Tune" in the "Parnell's Funeral and Other Poems" section of the new edition of *Poems*.[1]

The third major discrepancy between *A Full Moon in March* and the 1949 *Poems* occurs in the first of "Two Songs Rewritten for the Tune's Sake". As printed in the 1935 collection, the poem read as follows:

> That blonde girl there is my heart's desire,
> But I am shrunken to the bone,
> For all my toil has had for its hire
> Is drinking her health when lone, alone—
> *Aro, aro,*
> *Tomorrow night I will break in the door.*
>
> What is the good of a man if he
> Live lone, alone, with a speckled shin?
> O could I drink, my love on my knee,
> Between two barrels at the inn.
> *Aro, aro,*
> *To-morrow night I will break in the door.*

[1] At one point Yeats planned to include "Three Marching Songs" in *On the Boiler*. See the early set of page proofs in National Library of Ireland MS. 8771(8), where the songs are placed after the text of *Purgatory*.

The cross-reference in the 1949 *Poems* between "Three Songs to the Same Tune" and "Three Marching Songs", heretofore assigned to Yeats (as in VP 613), was doubtless the work of Mrs Yeats and/or Thomas Mark.

> Nine nights I lay and in longing sore
> Between two bushes under the rain;
> I had thought to have called her out to the door,
> But there I lay and I whistled in vain.
> *Aro, aro,*
> *Tomorrow night I will break in the door.*

This was considerably revised from the first version, published in the 1922 *Plays in Prose and Verse*, but Yeats was still not satisfied. He had another opportunity for revision when Macmillan decided to gather together a collection of *Nine One-Act Plays*, and he did not fail to seize it:

> My pretty Paistin is my heart's desire,
> Yet am I shrunken to skin and bone,
> For all that my heart has had for its hire
> Is what I can whistle alone and alone.
> *Aro, Aro.*
> *Tomorrow night I will break down the door.*
>
> What is the good of a man and he
> Alone and alone with a speckled shin?
> I would that I drank with my love on my knee,
> Between two barrels at the inn.
> *Aro, Aro.*
> *Tomorrow night I will break down the door.*
>
> Alone and alone nine nights I lay
> Between two bushes under the rain;
> I thought to have whistled her down that way,
> I whistled and whistled and whistled in vain.
> *Aro, Aro.*
> *Tomorrow night I will break down the door.*

However, Yeats apparently revised the poem still further. Among the "afterthoughts" which Mark sent to Mrs Yeats on 30 June 1939 was the following query:

> The new version of *Paistin Finn*. Is this text to be used in Vol. II of *Poems*: From 'A Full Moon in March' which now begins
>
>> That blonde girl there is my heart's desire?
>
> Also to be substituted in *Collected Plays*
>>   *Nine One-Act Plays?*

Mrs Yeats answered in the affirmative on all counts. I have not been able to locate the source of the changes which Mrs Yeats submitted for the 1949 *Poems*: this could have been a manuscript, a typescript, or, perhaps most likely, a corrected copy of *Nine One-Act Plays* (the single copy of that collection preserved in Yeats's library is unmarked). Nevertheless, I have decided to accept the new version in the new *Poems*. In this revision the refrain is modified to "*Oro, oro! / To-morrow night I will break down the door*" and its first line slightly indented; a comma is added in l. 8; and the poem has a new opening:

> My Paistin Finn is my sole desire,
> And I am shrunken to the bone,
> For all my heart has had for its hire
> Is what I can whistle alone and alone.

The remaining discrepancies between *A Full Moon in March* and the 1949 *Poems* involve matters of detail. Unfortunately, relatively little manuscript material for the volume appears to have survived. Although there are drafts of most of the poems in several notebooks, I have located only a very few typescripts and have found no proofs. With such slim evidence, it is often difficult to feel especially confident about a particular reading. In such instances I suggest that we should accept *A Full Moon in March* as the only version that Yeats is known to have approved — unless that text is so clearly corrupt that to preserve it would be to place the consistency of a given editorial policy ahead of the poems themselves. I list the variants below, giving the *Full Moon in March* reading followed by the 1949 *Poems* version, and citing what evidence does exist. The form used in the new *Poems* is asterisked.[2]

[2] This list does not include the variants in "Three Songs to the Same Tune", as the poem is not part of this section of the new *Poems*. I have also not listed here the variants in the second of the "Two Songs Rewritten for the Tune's Sake" found in *Nine One-Act Plays*, as it is clear that that edition reverts to the text of the 1934 *Collected Plays* and earlier printings. Lines 2–5 are moreover unique to *A Full Moon in March*.

The "Alternative Song for the Severed Head in 'The King of the Great Clock Tower'" was reprinted in *The Herne's Egg and Other Plays* (New York: Macmillan, 1938). It is unlikely that Yeats read proofs for that collection. In any event, the text of the poem is identical to that in *A Full Moon in March* except that the notation "Tune by Arthur Duff" is eliminated.

A. "Parnell's Funeral", II, l. 2. "Valera"/"Valéra"*

On 14 June 1939 Mrs Yeats sent Mark the change: "de Valéra (this is the way he writes the name itself)". Apparently de Valera was given to both forms, and in some letters from him to Yeats the accent is used in his signature. Moreover, on the final page proofs of *On the Boiler* Yeats added the accent mark in l. 18 of "A Statesman's Holiday".

B. "Alternative Song for the Severed Head in 'The King of the Great Clock Tower'", l. 6. *"mountain side"/"mountain-side"

Doubtless a correction by Mark.

C. Alternative Song for the Severed Head in 'The King of the Great Clock Tower'", l. 11. "Niam"/"Niamh"*

Yeats spelled the name variously "Niam", "Neave", and "Niamh". The change brings the spelling into conformity with the 1933 *Collected Poems* and seems an appropriate emendation.

D. "Ribh considers Christian Love insufficient", l. 2. *"wit;"/ "wit."

As the *Full Moon in March* reading agrees with the four earlier printings, it is unlikely that Yeats was responsible for the revision.

E. "What Magic Drum?", l. 5. "tongue,"/"tongue."*

As the extant typescript (in the collection of Michael B. Yeats) has no punctuation after "tongue", Yeats probably added it on the proofs for *A Full Moon in March*, in which case his mark might well have been misread. The contrast between the single, flowing sentence of the first stanza and the four sentences of the final stanza (three of them in the interrogative) seems important to the effect of the poem, so I have therefore accepted the emendation.

F. "Meru", l. 86. *"Greece"/"Greece,"

In revising the poem for *A Full Moon in March*, Yeats deleted one comma and added four others, including one in the same line ("good-bye, Rome!"); but he did not modify "Egypt and Greece good-bye".

Yeats described *A Full Moon in March* to Ethel Mannin as "a fragment of the past I had to get rid of" (L 843). With that and other work behind him, and determined to avoid the fate of

Wordsworth — "withering into eighty years, honoured and empty-witted" — Yeats produced an extraordinary collection of new poetry.[3] Harold Macmillan reminded Yeats on 21 June 1937 that "when you called here some time ago you mentioned that you were writing a good deal of poetry, and I wonder if perhaps you have sufficient to make a new volume for this year" (55896/224). As Macmillan explained their agreement to Watt on 22 June 1937, "Mr. Yeats will send us the material for a new volume of Lyrics which we shall publish in the spring of 1938. They will, however, first appear in one of the limited editions published by the Cuala Press" (55796/224). But with the inevitable delays, the Cuala Press was unable to publish *New Poems* until 18 May 1938; and Yeats's death intervened before a commercial edition could go forward.

The textual problems in this volume are formidable. Fortunately, the surviving manuscript materials are quite extensive. These include manuscripts and typescripts in the National Library of Ireland (MS. 13,593); some manuscripts and typescripts in the collection of Michael B. Yeats; the final corrected page proofs for *New Poems* in the collection of Michael B. Yeats; a corrected carbon typescript of "The Wild Old Wicked Man" from the R. A. Scott-James papers at the Humanities Research Center, University of Texas; and an early typescript of "A Model for the Laureate" and an early manuscript of "Those Images" from the Edith Shackleton Heald papers at Harvard University.[4] There is a copy of *New Poems* with numerous corrections by Yeats and inscribed "George from WBY" in the collection of Michael B. Yeats; and three copies of *Last Poems & Plays* with corrections by Mrs Yeats in the collection of Anne Yeats.

Michael B. Yeats's collection also includes a one-page typescript headed "Corrections to Yeats' Poems" and dated in pencil "March 1938", and a two-page typescript with the identical heading and dated in pencil "April 1938"; there is a copy of the

---

[3] *Mythologies* (London: Macmillan, 1959), p. 342.

[4] The Heald papers also include a typescript of "Ribh Prefers an Older Theology", which I did not cite in connection with *A Full Moon in March* as it is identical to the texts in the *London Mercury* (December 1934) and *The King of the Great Clock Tower* (Dublin: Cuala Press, 1934). More importantly, the Heald papers included a single sheet with holograph drafts of "Are You Content" on one side and "The Spirit Medium" on the other; this manuscript was not acquired by Harvard. My letter to the individual reported to own it has gone unanswered. Fortunately, there is a facsimile of "Are You Content" in the sale catalogue (Christie's, London, 5 July 1978, p. 33).

second list in the Scott-James papers. These lists were made by Mrs Yeats in connection with the printing of several of the lyrics from *New Poems* in the *London Mercury* in the spring of 1938.[5] Yeats had left Ireland for France on 8 January 1938, leaving Mrs Yeats to correspond with Scott-James, the editor of the *London Mercury*. On 17 January 1938 she sent him "the bunch of poems 2 copies of each he asked me to send you to choose from". On 27 January 1938 she wrote Scott-James that "it would probably save you time and trouble if I sent you WBY's corrected proofs (Cuala) of any poems you are using; I am sure you would be so kind as to correct the MERCURY proofs for him, yourself". However, on 31 January 1938 Mrs Yeats told him "WBY returned to me only one copy of his corrected proofs and did not return the typescript. I have therefore made notes of corrections; they are mostly punctuation". Scott-James acknowledged the corrections on 2 February 1938 and promised to "have proofs sent to you to Mentone when they are ready".[6] Since Yeats had the opportunity to read proofs for both the *London Mercury* and the Cuala volume (the printing of which was not completed until 9 April 1938) after Mrs Yeats had prepared her lists of "Corrections to Yeats's Poems", it is understandable that neither the *London Mercury* nor the *New Poems* texts incorporate all of the changes on the lists.

A final item in the collection of Michael B. Yeats is a three-page manuscript by Mrs Yeats headed "Notes on '*A Note on the Texts*'". As it refers to the Macmillan edition of *Last Poems & Plays*, it must have been written after January 1940. I suspect that it is related to the 1949 *Poems*, even though that edition did not include a "*A Note on the Texts*".[7]

---

[5] The March 1938 list includes all of the poems published in the *London Mercury* for that month except "The Old Stone Cross" and "To a Friend". However, the title "To a Friend" is typed at the bottom of the page, so apparently a second sheet has been lost or misfiled. The April 1938 list includes all four of the poems that appeared in the *London Mercury* for that month.

[6] Letters to and from R. A. Scott-James are quoted with the permission of the Humanities Research Center of the University of Texas and Mrs Paula Scott-James.

[7] It is also possible that Mrs Yeats's "Notes" are connected with the Scribner Edition, which was not cancelled until 1953.

Another small uncertainty about "Notes" involves the comment on "A Nativity": "Yeats altered *gnat* to *moth* deliberately. He thought *gnat* created a wrong image. He said to me 'No! One *swats* gnats & mosquitoes–'". Since all manuscripts and published editions read "What brushes fly and moth aside?" (l. 7), the point of Mrs Yeats's remark is unclear – unless, say, Mark had queried the line and suggested that "moth" was a misprint for "gnat".

The textual problems in *New Poems* are further complicated by a statement which Mrs Yeats made to Thomas Mark in a letter of 17 April 1939. Sending him the material for the second volume of *Poems* in the Coole Edition, she wrote as follows:

> I send you "New Poems" (published by the Cuala Press in April, 1938) and "Last Poems" (to be published at the end of May). All these poems were very carefully revised in France last winter, and, although you will probably find points to raise on the typescripts, they *are* final versions.

Mark acknowledged the receipt of this material on 18 April 1939 (55822/412), and on 21 April 1939 he wrote Mrs Yeats that "I hope to be able to go through the typescript of "New Poems" and "Last Poems" this weekend, and the material can then be sent to the printers for the edition de luxe. I will see that you receive proofs of both volumes of poems, with any queries I may have to raise, before they go to the printers for press" (55822/550).

The crucial point here is Mrs Yeats's implication that Yeats revised some typescripts of *New Poems* in the last months of his life. If this were so, it would be possible to accept the numerous emendations made for *Last Poems & Plays* as authorial. However, I believe that Mrs Yeats's statement about revisions on typescripts refers only to *Last Poems* and not to *New Poems*. First, once a volume was in print, it was Yeats's habit to make whatever revisions he wanted in a copy, usually marking it "corrected"; it would have been atypical for him to have bypassed the printed *New Poems* in favour of the older typescripts (or to have new typescripts prepared). Secondly, if such corrected typescripts existed, Mrs Yeats would surely have preserved them; yet there is no such material in either the National Library of Ireland or the collection of Michael B. Yeats. Rather, I am convinced that the typescripts sent to Mark were the corrected typescripts used as copy for *New Poems* and that it was only after forwarding the material that she discovered the numerous corrections Yeats had made in the copy of *New Poems* inscribed "George from WBY". These unusually clean typescripts are now divided between the National Library of Ireland and the collection of Michael B. Yeats.

In the new *Poems* I have thus used the corrected copy of *New Poems* as the basic text. I suspect that, especially in terms of punctuation, many readers will regret the absence of the more regularised texts that appeared in *Last Poems & Plays* and, with a few more changes, in the 1949 *Poems*. However, I think we must recall that Yeats came to *New Poems* and *Last Poems* directly from the immersion in contemporary poetry involved in compiling *The Oxford Book of Modern Verse*. Certainly the "irregularity" of his punctuation is no more radical than that found in much of the verse of his own age. To cite two examples from the *Oxford Book*, consider the opening of T. S. Eliot's "The Hollow Men":

> We are the hollow men
> We are the stuffed men
> Leaning together
> Headpiece filled with straw. Alas!
> Our dried voices, when
> We whisper together
> Are quiet and meaningless
> As wind in dry grass
> Or rats' feet over broken glass
> In our dry cellar[.]

Or, a poem with which Yeats was doubtless more familiar, Margot Ruddock's "I take thee Life":

> I take thee, Life,
> Because I need,
> A wanton love
> My flesh to feed.
>
> But still my soul
> Insatiate
> Cries out, cries out
> For its true mate.[8]

Furthermore, as Thomas Parkinson has brilliantly argued in *W. B. Yeats: The Later Poetry*, Yeats's poems after *A Full Moon in March* display "a genuine effort to break free, a persistent drive toward an idiom that would allow him to keep from merely repeating his already richly elaborated set of icons".[9] Parkinson sees this

[8] *The Oxford Book of Modern Verse* (Oxford: Clarendon Press, 1936), pp. 285, 418.
[9] *W. B. Yeats: The Later Poetry*, p. 177. See esp. pp. 168–80 and 228–31.

spirit of liberation in terms of inconography and prosody, but I would suggest that it applies with equal force to Yeats's punctuation. At the least, I think we must hesitate before changing something which Yeats is known to have read and to have approved. Perhaps in the last analysis we must, to paraphrase Henry James, "grant the poet his punctuation".

The list below includes all of the changes that Yeats made in the corrected copy of *New Poems*. Of the posthumous emendations made by Mrs Yeats and Thomas Mark, I have cited the few which have been admitted into the new *Poems* as well as those for which some evidence survives. It seemed of little point simply to list the substantial number of remaining emendations, which in all likelihood were first suggested by Mark and then accepted by Mrs Yeats (interested readers can of course recover these emendations from the *Variorum Poems*).

"Lapis Lazuli"
There are four alterations in the corrected copy of *New Poems*:

12: Yeats added the comma after "there".
41: Yeats added the comma after "serving-man".
52: Yeats changed the semi-colon to a period.
54: Yeats changed the semi-colon to a period.

In her "Note on '*A Note on the Texts*'", Mrs Yeats justified the punctuation of the final two lines:

> Deliberate punctuation by WB who read the two lines
>   Their eyes mid many wrinkles, their eyes[,]
>   Their ancient, glittering eyes, are gay.
> (Glittering eyes and gay read on a higher note.)

"Sweet Dancer"
In the corrected copy of *New Poems* Yeats added the missing line 4: "Escaped from her bitter youth". The line is also lacking in the April 1938 "Corrections to Yeats's Poems", where the entire first stanza has been typed out. In her "Notes on '*A Note on the Texts*'", Mrs Yeats explained that the poem had been "corrected in Macmillan ed.", but there is no support for the comma after

"away" (l. 9) other than the early version sent to Dorothy Wellesley;[10] and none at all for the italics and the comma after the
initial "Ah" in the refrains.

"The Three Bushes"
There are two changes in the corrected copy of *New Poems*:

  1: Yeats added the comma at the end of the line.
  31: Yeats added the comma at the end of the line.

"The Lady's Second Song"
In the corrected copy of *New Poems*, Yeats altered the misprint
"breast" to "beast" (l. 18), the reading of the final corrected
carbon typescript in the National Library of Ireland. The version
in *New Poems* otherwise follows that typescript exactly. There is
thus no support for the additional commas in ll. 3, 5, and 19 found
in the 1940 Macmillan edition. Although Jon Stallworthy apparently considers these nothing more than "minor differences of
punctuation", I would suggest that the first − at least − is significant.[11] "What matter, we are but women" implies the speaker's
acceptance of women as subservient; the proper "What matter we
are but women" suggests almost precisely the opposite.

"The Chambermaid's First Song"
In the list of queries which Thomas Mark sent to Mrs Yeats in April
1949, he asked "Should there be a query after 'sigh for,' as for the
preceding question?" In fact, the question mark in l. 4 had only
been introduced in *Last Poems & Plays*; but Mrs Yeats overlooked
that and agreed with the suggestion. Although the final typescript
of the poem has not survived (the corrected carbon typescript in
the National Library of Ireland is unpunctuated save for the final
period), the *New Poems* text follows precisely the corrected page

----

[10] *Letters on Poetry from W. B. Yeats to Dorothy Wellesley*, intro. Kathleen
Raine (London: Oxford University Press, 1964), p. 120. Hereafter cited LDW.
Although I refer to these letters in connection with the texts in *New Poems*, I
have no great faith in the accuracy of the transcriptions provided in the published edition. Unfortunately, John Kelly, General Editor of the forthcoming
Collected Letters of W. B. Yeats, has so far been unable to acquire copies of
the original letters.

[11] Jon Stallworthy, *Vision and Revision in Yeats's* Last Poems (Oxford:
Clarendon Press, 1969), p. 100.

proofs for the volume. The version sent to Dorothy Wellesley in 1936 includes a comma at l. 4 but not at l. 5.

"An Acre of Grass"
There are two changes in the corrected copy of *New Poems*:

4: Yeats changed the comma to a semi-colon.
22: Yeats changed the comma to a semi-colon.

That these revisions represent Yeats's change of mind rather than the correction of misprints in *New Poems* is confirmed not only by the proofs for that edition but also by the April 1938 "Corrections to Yeats's Poems", where commas are indicated for both lines.

"What Then?"
I have added the comma in "wife, daughter" (l. 12), bringing the poem into conformity with both the final corrected typescript in the National Library of Ireland and the printing in *The Erasmian* (Dublin) for April 1937.

"A Crazed Girl"
The text in *New Poems* is identical to the final corrected carbon typescript in the National Library of Ireland (except for the lack of quotation marks in l. 14) and thus no emendations have been admitted. However, the quotation from Margot Ruddock, "O sea-starved hungry sea", was the subject of an amusing exchange between Mark and Mrs Yeats. When Mrs Yeats returned the proofs of the second volume of *Poems* to Mark on 14 June 1939, she responded to one of his suggestions as follows: "'sea-starved' looks very odd. A dash instead of hyphen as you suggest". But Mark was still dissatisfied with the line. Included in the "afterthoughts" which he sent Mrs Yeats on 30 June 1939 was the following remark:

'A Crazed Girl'. 'O sea − starved hungry sea'[.] 'starved hungry' sounds odd, and in the night I decided the MS. might have '*sex*-starved'. By daylight it seems less probable.

Mrs Yeats's response, sent to him on 5 July 1939, was "comma after starved? The line is correct". Mark went ahead and made the change, and we find in *Last Poems & Plays*, "O sea−starved, hungry sea". However, as Mark was to indicate on the 14 June 1939 list of corrections, "Mrs. Yeats changed this later". Thus in the 1949 *Poems* we are given "O sea-starved, hungry sea", a change which Mrs Yeats also made in two of her corrected copies of *Last Poems & Plays*. Nevertheless, as the precise line is unique to "A Crazed Girl", Margot Ruddock herself having written only "Sea-starved, hungry sea", I have seen no reason to emend Yeats's version.[12]

"To Dorothy Wellesley"

In the corrected copy of *New Poems*, Yeats changed the title "To a Friend" to "To Dorothy Wellesley". Otherwise the text follows precisely the final corrected typescript in the collection of Michael B. Yeats.

"The Curse of Cromwell"

There are two revisions in the corrected copy of *New Poems*:

9: Yeats added the comma.
21: Yeats added the comma.

As this is one of the most heavily emended poems in the collection, perhaps it should be added that *New Poems* follows the final typescript in the collection of Michael B. Yeats in all respects except the following: (1) the last three refrains on the typescript are separated by a space from the stanzas; (2) the typescript has a comma after "account" (l. 12) rather than a period; (3) the typescript reads "swordsman" (l. 20) rather than "swordsmen". The final proofs are identical with the text in *New Poems*.

"The O'Rahilly"

In the corrected copy of *New Poems* Yeats changed the comma after "Henry Street" (l. 31) to a semi-colon.

"The Wild Wicked Old Man"

As this is another heavily emended poem, perhaps it should be pointed out that *New Poems* follows the final corrected typescript in the Scott-James papers in all but three respects: (1) the typescript has a period after "hills" (l. 2) rather than a comma; (2) the typescript has a period after "wills" (l. 4) rather than a comma; and (3) the typescript has a comma after "light" (l. 38) rather than

[12] Margot Ruddock, *The Lemon Tree* (London: J. M. Dent, 1937), p. 9.

no punctuation. The revisions were made before the final proofs of the volume, which are identical with the printed text.

"The Spur"
The *London Mercury* for March 1938 printed l. 2 as "Should dance attention upon my old age". The correct reading appeared in *New Poems*: "Should dance attendance upon my old age". For reasons inexplicable to me, *Last Poems & Plays* reverts to "attention", even though the versions sent to Ethel Mannin (L 872) and Dorothy Wellesley (LDW 110) in December 1936, the early manuscripts and typescripts in the National Library of Ireland, and the final corrected typescript in the collection of Michael B. Yeats all read "attendance". Yeats would hardly have sacrificed the vivid image of lust and range as courtiers to the aged poet.[13]

"The Pilgrim"
The italics on the refrains were suggested by Mrs Yeats to Mark on 14 June 1939. *New Poems* follows the final typescript in the collection of Michael B. Yeats in not using italics.

"Colonel Martin"
In the corrected copy of *New Poems*, Yeats added the comma after "abed" (l. 31). Otherwise *New Poems* follows the final typescript in the collection of Michael B. Yeats except for two revisions: (1) ll. 68–9 of the typescript read "My grand-dad saw with his own eyes / Those words come out true in the end," rather than "And want he did; for my own grand-dad / Saw the story's end,"; and (2) the typescript uses the spelling "jewellery" (ll. 21, 33) rather than "jewelry". In her letter to Mark on 17 April 1939 Mrs Yeats explained that "jewelry is deliberately spelt that way because it is an older form than the modern jewellery", information which must have come to Yeats while he was correcting the proofs for *New Poems*.

Also of some interest is Mrs Yeats's comment on the refrain of the poem, which in its first printing in *A Broadside* (Dec. 1937) had read "Lullabulloo, buloo, buloo, lullabulloo, bullo". On her "Notes on '*A Note on the Texts*'", Mrs Yeats explained "refrain as in 'Last Poems' & Macmillan ed. is the *original* version. The longer

---

[13] Stallworthy also argues in favour of "attendance" in *Vision and Revision*, p. 102.

one was really created by F. R. Higgins for purposes of singing. I
persuaded WBY to replace the original in [?] 1938".

"The Municipal Gallery Re-visited"

In the corrected copy of *New Poems*, Yeats made but one change,
adding the comma after "Augusta Gregory" (l. 41). However, as
this poem was the subject of an extensive collaboration between
Mrs Yeats and Mark, it is perhaps necessary to demonstrate the
essential similarity of the *New Poems* version with the final carbon
typescript in the National Library of Ireland. The differences
between the typescript and the *New Poems* version are as follows:

> 14: the typescript offers no punctuation after "way" instead of
> the period.
> 15: the typescript reads "I met her more than fifty years ago"
> rather than "I met her all but fifty years ago".
> 21: the typescript has a semi-colon after "son" rather than a
> comma.
> 22: the typescript reads "Lane − "onlie begetter" of all these−"
> rather than "Lane, "onlie begetter" of all these;".
> 26−7: the typescript reads ""Since Rembrandt there has been
> none greater" Synge / Declared, and a great portrait certainly;"
> rather than ""Greatest since Rembrandt," according to John
> Synge; / A great ebullient portrait certainly;".
> 40: the typescript reads "−An image out of Spenser and the
> common tongue−" rather than "(An image out of Spenser and
> the common tongue)".
> 48: the typescript reads "And here's John Synge, a meditative
> man", rather than "And here's John Synge himself, that rooted
> man".
> 52: the typescript reads "therein" rather than "thereon".

The text of the poem which appeared in *A Speech and Two
Poems*, a small booklet issued in December 1937 to commemorate
the Irish Academy of Letters Banquet on 17 August 1937, is
apparently intermediate between the typescript and the version in
New Poems. The final proofs for *New Poems* are identical with the
printed text.

After Mrs Yeats had sent the typescripts of *New Poems* and *Last
Poems* to Mark on 17 April 1939, she came across the following
letter from John Sparrow to Yeats on 5 August 1938:

Blackwells wrote to me to say that they know of no translation of any of the work of Stefan Georg. They would know if any did exist.

So nothing can be done.

I have been reading *New Poems* again, with even increased enjoyment.

The small point which I think I mentioned to you occurs at the join between stanzas V and VI of *The Municipal Gallery Re-Visited*. If the "image" is the image of fox and badger, the sequence of thought would be better expressed, I think, by a — after "swept" and a full stop after "tongue".

Yeats marked this letter "answered" and then, if he followed his usual habits, doubtless inserted it into the corrected copy of *New Poems*, which is where I conjecture Mrs Yeats discovered it (and where it remains today, in the collection of Michael B. Yeats). She wrote to Sparrow on 27 April 1939 as follows:

I have a letter of yours dated 5.8.38 which has been marked 'answered' by WBY. It is about the punctuation of THE MUNI-CIPAL GALLERY RE-VISITED. Personally I entirely agree with your punctuation of the last line of stanza V & the first line of VI; but WBY may have written some alternative suggestion to you? I would be greatly obliged if you would let me know about this, & also if you have any other suggestions of a similar kind. I am now correcting proofs of poems for vols. 1 & 2 (POEMS) for the forthcoming collected edition.

Mrs Yeats went on to inform Sparrow about the misprints in *New Poems* in "Sweet Dancer" and "The Lady's Song" and concluded "I enclose typed copy of MUNICIPAL GALLERY on which you might mark punctuation".

Sparrow replied to Mrs Yeats on 29 April 1939, quoting from Yeats's letter to him (since lost or misplaced): "W.B.Y. wrote to me, on the 30th August 1938, in answer to the letter you quote, 'I thank you very much for your correction in the punctuation of my poem. I shall remember it when I next correct the proof sheets' — so I think the correction has his sanction."[14]

In fact, Yeats's reply is about as ambivalent as can be imagined:

[14] I am indebted to John Sparrow for a copy of Mrs Yeats's letter to him and for permission to quote from his letters.

he does not promise to "make" the correction but simply to "remember" it. As Yeats was in Riversdale when he wrote to Sparrow, he had ample opportunity to make the change in the corrected copy of *New Poems* (which already had been revised in the following line). But the fact that he did not suggests that either he was contemplating a substantial revision of the stanzas in question or that he was satisfied with the punctuation as printed in *New Poems*.

Mrs Yeats and Thomas Mark were not content, however, and so in *Last Poems & Plays* the passage appears as

> No fox can foul the lair the badger swept.
> VI
> (An image out of Spenser and the common tongue.)

Nor were they finished emending "The Municipal Gallery Revisited". Mrs Yeats wrote to Mark a decade later, on 8 April 1949, as follows:

> There are some corrections in LAST POEMS. I send a copy; will you go through them and let me know what you think. I am not sure about page 49. Line 7 stanza V has a full stop. I have deleted the full stop and made a note to put the full stop of line 1 Stanza VI *outside* the bracket. Should there be a dash after the line
>
> No fox can foul the lair the badger swept"?
> Certainly a full stop is wrong.
> Page 49. You will have noticed that in the re-writing of stanza V WBY has seven lines instead of eight. Do you think that a note should be made about this, giving the original stanza?

In his response, Mark suggested "I think it would be best to have a dash after 'swept' and to move the full stop after 'tongue' outside the bracket as you suggest". He also noted the misprint of "Griffiths" (l. 4), unique to the 1940 Macmillan edition, and he made two further suggestions for revision. He asked "do you think there should be a semi-colon after 'blessed' [l. 8], as the list is continued in v. II?"; and "semi-colon after 'all' [l. 24], for the same reason?" When Mrs Yeats returned the list of queries to Mark on 29 April 1949, she agreed to all of his suggestions, and thus the changes were made for the 1949 *Poems*. The passage of the greatest debate reads

No fox can foul the lair the badger swept—
VI
(An image out of Spenser and the common tongue).

In the added note, heretofore wrongly ascribed to Yeats (as in VP 838—9), the version of the fifth stanza provided is taken from *A Speech and Two Poems*.

I have dwelled on this episode at length because it is a paradigm of the fate of Yeats's poems after his death. There was essentially no attempt to verify the poems by examining the manuscripts; rather, they were simply regularised, more or less according to the rules of prose. Furthermore, in this particular instance, Mrs Yeats's correspondence with John Sparrow supports my earlier conjecture that there were not any typescripts of *New Poems* corrected by Yeats in the winter of 1938.

A full comparison of "The Municipal Gallery Re-visited" as Yeats wrote it and as Mrs Yeats and Thomas Mark emended it is, I trust, unnecessary, but perhaps some brief comments are in order. Take, for example, what might appear as the straightforward "correction" of the punctuation of l. 8 from a period (as in all texts before 1949) to a semi-colon. Here we must distinguish between the paintings which doubtless inspired the poem and the paintings as they are transformed *within the poem*. That is, Yeats's "The Municipal Gallery Re-visited" gives us two separate paintings, not one:

A revolutionary soldier kneeling to be blessed.
II
An Abbot or Archbishop with an upraised hand
Blessing the Tricolour.

Now Yeats was not so ignorant of church regalia as to mistake the mitred figure of John Lavery's *The Blessing of the Colours* for an "Abbot"![15] But the subtle irony of his making two pictures out of one has not, I think, been noticed. That is, within the poem the blessing is given only to the emblem of the state and not to the person who symbolises those who created it; the Church, in other words, looks the other way when confronted with the fact of violence but condones and accepts the results of that violence.

---

[15] See the reproduction in Arland Ussher, *Yeats at the Municipal Gallery* (Dublin: Charlmont House, 1959), p. [4].

Recall that Yeats was the author of a poem called "Church and State" and that he wrote in *A Speech and Two Poems* that "in those rooms of the Municipal Gallery I saw Ireland in spiritual freedom . . ." (VP 840).

As for the seventh stanza, I would argue that throughout "The Municipal Gallery Re-visited" Yeats is exploiting the tension between the strict ottava rima form and an interior monologue in which, "Heart smitten with emotion" and "in despair", he reviews the past not only of Ireland but also of himself, and particularly of his relationship with two of the central figures in his life and art — the dual concerns being joined in "Ireland's history in their lineaments trace". It is thus appropriate that the ottava rima form should be broken in that stanza which admits the death of Lady Gregory, whom Yeats once described — in a private diary and without exaggeration or sentimentality — as "mother, friend, sister and brother".[16] It is absurd, I suggest, to assume that Yeats was simply unable to compose an eighth line for the stanza (or that "Of all that scholarly generations had held dear" was altogether unacceptable).

Finally, the enjambment between the fifth and sixth stanzas is itself a reassertion of the poetic tradition, a reminder to Yeats that, as the only living member of the artistic triumvirate, it is his responsibility to preserve and extend that tradition. The "scholarly" annotation citing Spenser, the parenthesis taking the place of a footnote, serves the same function. Indeed, by the very composition of "The Municipal Gallery Re-visited", Yeats is ensuring that Synge and Lady Gregory will not meet the fate of the Earl of Leicester. As printed in his own *Poems of Spenser* (1906),

> He now is gone, the whiles the Foxe is crept
> Into the hole, the which the Badger swept.
>
> He now is gone, and all his glorie gone,
> And all his greatness vapoured to nought,
> That as a glasse upon the water shone,
> Which vanisht quite, so soone as it was sought:
> His name is worn alreadie out of thought,

[16] *Memoirs*, ed. Denis Donoghue (London: Macmillan, 1972), pp. 160–1. The passage continues "I cannot realize the world without her — she brought to my wavering thoughts steadfast nobility. All day long the thought of losing her is like a conflagration in the rafters. Friendship is all the house I have" (p. 161).

Ne anie Poet seekes him to revive,
Yet manie Poets honoured him alive.[17]

"Are You Content"
There are three revisions in the corrected copy of *New Poems*:

1: Yeats added the comma after "son".
9: Yeats changed the spelling "Drumcliffe" to "Drumcliff".
15: Yeats added the comma after "back".

I have also admitted one emendation in "Are You Content", removing the apostrophe from "Butlers" (l. 15). This was included in both periodical texts and in *New Poems*, as well as on the April 1938 "Corrections to Yeats's Poems". It is lacking, however, on the final corrected typescript in the National Library of Ireland.

[17] "The Death of the Earl of Leicester", *Poems of Spenser* (Edinburgh: T. C. & E. C. Jack, 1906), p. 72. Cf. Yeats's statement in the Introduction that "the lamentation over the Earl of Leicester's death is more than a conventional Ode to a dead patron" (p. xvii).

CHAPTER FIVE

Last Poems

When Yeats died he had in print eight new poems, in the December 1938 and January 1939 issues of the *London Mercury*; five of these had also appeared in America, in *The Nation* for 10 December 1938 and the January 1939 *Atlantic Monthly*.[1] A further three poems were at the press in *On the Boiler*, for which Yeats had read proof.[2] Eleven additional poems were also unpublished. Six of these were thereafter printed in various periodicals, beginning with "Under Ben Bulben" in the Irish press on 3 February 1939 and ending with "Three Songs to the One Burden" in the *Spectator* for 26 May 1939. The remaining five poems were first published in *Last Poems and Two Plays*, issued by the Cuala Press in an edition of five hundred copies on 10 July 1939; this gathering did not contain the poems from *On the Boiler*. In January of 1940, Macmillan, London, published 2000 copies of *Last Poems & Plays*; this included the lyrics from both *New Poems* and *Last Poems and Two Plays*, as well as the poems from *On the Boiler*. This volume was also published on 14 May 1940 by Macmillan, New York.

As these facts suggest, the textual problems presented by *Last Poems* are enormous. Fortunately, though, the most visible and most discussed problem, can be resolved.

[1] The British Library copy of the December 1938 *London Mercury* was received on 1 December 1938, the January 1939 issue on 30 December 1938. At least the earlier issue reached Yeats in France, as he wrote Scott-James on 29 December 1938 that "The Christmas Mercury has just arrived". However, there are no copies of either issue preserved in his library.

[2] See Sandra F. Siegel, "Yeats's Quarrel with Himself: The Design and Argument of *On the Boiler*", *Bulletin of Research in the Humanities*, 81, No. 3 (Autumn 1978), 349–68, esp. 352–3. Unfortunately, Siegel was unaware of the second and later set of page proofs with Yeats's corrections in British Library Additional Manuscripts 55881.

In *Yeats at His Last* (p. 47, n. 8) Stanley Sultan had speculated that Yeats would have received "at least galleys" but could offer no firm evidence.

One of the last things that Yeats wrote was a table of contents for an untitled volume. *Last Poems and Two Plays* follows this list in all respects. As the list includes "The Black Tower", the typescript of which is dated 21 January 1939, it must have been composed within, say, the last two weeks of Yeats's life. Curtis Bradford's conjecture that there was no authority for the different order and contents in *Last Poems & Plays* can now be confirmed. When Thomas Mark sent Mrs Yeats the proofs for the second volume of *Poems* on 8 June 1939, he must have suggested that "Under Ben Bulben" might be moved from the beginning of the *Last Poems* section to the end. Mrs Yeats replied on 14 June 1939 as follows:

> Certainly put 'Under Ben Bulben' at the end of the volume. Its present position was WBY's, but I t[h]ink now it should undoubtedly be at the end as you suggest.

Likewise, in a letter to Harold Macmillan on the same day, she told him that "'Purgatory' should precede 'The Death of Cuchulain' of course", again going against the draft table of contents and the order of *Last Poems and Two Plays*, the printing of which had just been completed.

In addition to placing "Under Ben Bulben" at the end of the volume, the Macmillan edition (of course followed in the 1949 *Poems*) offers a radical rearrangement of the other poems. Compared to the authorised scheme, the works are in the following order: 2, 6–8, 5, 9–11, 13, 12, 14–16, the three poems from *On the Boiler* (themselves reordered 1, 3, 2), 18–19, 17, 4, 3, 1. How that order was arrived at is anyone's guess: mine is that it was suggested by Mark and approved by Mrs Yeats.

There are three other major defects in *Last Poems & Plays*. First, there is clearly no reason to include the lyrics from *On the Boiler*, as Yeats deliberately left them off his draft table of contents. Secondly, the volume artificially yokes together *New Poems* and *Last Poems*. As with *The Winding Stair and Other Poems* being an offshoot of the *Collected Poems*, the concept of *Last Poems & Plays* came not from Yeats but from his publishers. When Mark received the typescripts for *New Poems* and *Last Poems*, he obviously realised that there was sufficient material for a new volume. He wrote to Mrs Yeats on 21 April 1939, "I believe I am right in thinking that you will be sending us the text of 'Purgatory' and 'The Death of Cuchulain' for the *separate* edition of

these poems, and that the volume is to appear under the title of
"Last Poems and Plays"'" (55822/550). Mark was doubtless re-
membering correctly his discussion with Mrs Yeats on 17 March
1939, but she seems to have ignored his query. Instead, on 7 June
1939 she sent Mark copies not only of *Purgatory* and *The Death of
Cuchulain* but also of *The Herne's Egg* (which had been published
in 1938). Mark evidently took it that she was suggesting a separate
book of the three plays. On 13 June 1939, Harold Macmillan informed Mrs Yeats that the plays were too short for an edition and
that "I suggest a volume to be entitled "Last Poems and Plays",
which we could issue this autumn" (55825/303). Mrs Yeats at last
indicated her agreement to this proposal in a letter of 14 June
1939. In short, the Cuala Press *Last Poems and Two Plays* was too
slim for a commercial edition; Macmillan had been promised *New
Poems* but had not yet published it. Thus was born *Last Poems &
Plays*.

The final major problem with the 1940 collection is the very
title, "Last Poems". Stanley Sultan has recently argued that since
the list of Cuala Press publications in the first edition of *On the
Boiler* ([1939]) includes *Last Poems*, that title "is no editor's catch-
all" but carries "the living poet's authority".[3] However, a close
examination of the advertisement clearly suggests that the entry
for *Last Poems* was a late addition: "LAST POEMS W. B.
YEATS" is crammed on to one line and is all in large capitals,
whereas all of the other books are given two different type sizes and
two or more lines, as in "NEW POEMS: / By W. B. Yeats".
Although Yeats had informed Elizabeth Pelham on 4 January 1939
that "I know for certain my time will not be long" (L 922), I do not
believe that he was indeed convinced that the poems listed on the
table of contents were his "Last Poems". As we have noted, the
table of contents is itself untitled, as was Yeats's usual practice in
such draft lists. Based on the titles of his previous volumes, particularly of his Cuala Press editions, I am convinced that had he

---

[3] *Yeats at His Last*, p. 20. Curtis Bradford, who had the advantage of conversa-
tions with Mrs Yeats, wrote of the title that "I do not know its source" (*Yeats's
'Last Poems' Again*, p. 259).

Mrs Yeats informed Wade that "only about four copies" of the first edition of
On the Boiler "had been issued when it was decided to reprint the book; the
whole remainder of the edition was then destroyed and the new edition sub-
stituted" (*Bibliography*, p. 201). I know of two surviving copies, one in the collection of Michael B. Yeats and the other in the Wesleyan University Library. I
am indebted to Michael Durkan for sending me a copy of the latter.

lived to see the volume through the press the title would have been something on the order of *Under Ben Bulben: Poems and Two Plays* or perhaps simply *Under Ben Bulben*.[4] However, as I can find no direct evidence to support my belief, in the new *Poems* I have adopted (reluctantly) the heading "[Last Poems]". In all other respects, the new edition follows *New Poems* and *Last Poems and Two Plays* in contents and order.

Once past these matters, though, the textual problems in *Last Poems* are not so easily resolved. One general concern is the question of differences in the poems in periodicals between British and American printings, something which had plagued Yeats as early as his first book published in America, *John Sherman and Dhoya*.[5] In the case of the lyrics in *Last Poems*, it is clear that it was R. A. Scott-James who was responsible for placing the poems in American journals, a task he had also performed for some of the works in *New Poems*. I conjecture that Yeats offered Scott-James a substantial number of poems for the *London Mercury* when they lunched together sometime in September 1938.[6] Mrs Yeats wrote to Scott-James on 1 November 1938, asking "May I have back

---

[4] Writing to F. R. Higgins on 24 December 1938 about future publications by the Cuala Press, Yeats explained that "I could let you have a volume of poems but it would of course be very much better if some other name could come in first". Unfortunately for our purposes, he did not supply Higgins with the title of the projected volume. Yeats's letter to Higgins are held by the Humanities Research Center of the University of Texas. I am grateful to John Kelly for calling my attention to them.

[5] In my edition of *John Sherman and Dhoya* (Detroit: Wayne State University Press, 1969), pp. 32–3, I noted some substantive differences between the English and American editions and stated that "the reason for these and other variants between the two 1891 printings must remain open to question," as indeed it still does. My speculation was, and remains, that Yeats prepared two separate manuscripts of the work.

[6] In *W. B. Yeats, 1865–1939*, 2nd ed. (London: Macmillan, 1962), p. 473, Joseph Hone notes that "in September [1938] he was off once again to his friends in Sussex. He spent a day at Oxford, and driving with Miss Heald from there to Steyning, stopped at R. A. Scott-James' cottage in Berkshire to lunch, read his recent poems, and to talk about Spender, Charles Madge and George Barker." Yeats had written Heald on 4 September 1938 that "when we meet at the end of this month or thereabouts I shall have much poetry to read to you" (L 915). Yeats was back in Dublin by 8 October 1938 (L 916). He had returned to England, now on his way to France, by 30 October 1938 (LDW 190). Incidentally, the date of 9 October 1938 for Yeats's letter in LDW 189 must be an error; the letter should date from 1937, as indicated by the reference to a broadcast on 29 October ("My Own Poetry Again"), and should be moved to LDW 146.

copies of the poems you do not want to use in THE MERCURY out of the bunch I sent you two or three weeks ago?" She also wrote that "I wired you today saying 'yes please arrange for America'. I thought WBY had arranged this with you when you were talking together." As she had done with *New Poems*, Mrs Yeats doubtless sent him two copies of each poem.

Scott-James used five of the poems he had received in his December 1938 issue, also placing two of them in *The Nation* for 10 December 1938, where they appeared "by arrangement with the London *Mercury*" (VP 621, 623 [corrected]), and the other three in *The New Republic* for 15 February 1939.[7] He then printed three more lyrics in the January 1939 volume, and he also placed them in the *Atlantic Monthly* of the same month. The fact that these poems are in precisely the same order as in *Last Poems and Two Plays* suggests that at least part of the order of that collection was clear in Yeats's mind some months before he drafted the table of contents.

It is not altogether clear why no Yeats poems appeared in the *London Mercury* for February 1938. On 29 December 1938 Yeats wrote to Scott-James to ask "Would you please send me here any typed copies of poems of mine which you have and are not going to use; I want to put in order the contents of a new volume, and I shall not be able to get copies from home until my wife returns there in a few weeks time". On 11 January 1939, Yeats wrote to "Thank you for your letter of January 2nd enclosing copies of poems. Would you very kindly send me to the above address 'His Convictions' and 'Three Songs to the One Burden'. I will return copies in case you care to use them in May, but I have made a number of alterations in the 'Three Songs'." Yeats added that the Cuala volume would not be published until May. My guess is that when Scott-James returned the poems he did not want on 2 January 1939, he also told Yeats that he was keeping a number of others for future publication and needed to know when the Cuala edition would appear. In any event, Yeats's death on 28 January obviously complicated whatever plans Scott-James may have had. As Mrs Yeats explained to him in a letter of 18 February 1939,

I published the poem originally called "His Convictions" and

---

[7] This date is deceiving. *The New Republic* had agreed to publish the poems well before 4 January 1939, as on that day Scott-James's secretary forwarded their royalty payments to Mrs Yeats.

re-named by him on the Thursday morning before he died "Under Ben Bulben" (in his own writing on the typescript which you had returned to him a little time before) because there had been some activity in Dublin to have a burial at St. Patrick's Cathedral; I decided to use that poem to ensure that this activity should not continue. After that publication in the 3 daily newspapers no one in Ireland could decently press what was against his own written wishes.

Likewise, I doubt that Scott-James ever received the corrected copy of "Three Songs to the One Burden" which Yeats had promised him. The poem was eventually placed by Yeats's agent in *The Spectator* for 26 May 1939.[8] However, in that same letter Mrs Yeats also noted that "I found your letter on my return from Sligo last Saturday Feb 11th, and I wired to you at your private address to go ahead with the poems you had as I could not send you copies of the two last poems in time for March 'MERCURY'". Thus four more poems by Yeats were published in the March 1939 issue, also appearing in America in either *The Nation* or *The New Republic*.[9]

For the lyrics printed in the December 1938 and January 1939 numbers of the *London Mercury*, Yeats had the opportunity to correct proofs, as he had done earlier in 1938 for some works from *New Poems*. He was in England during the production of the December 1938 issue, and as soon as he arrived in France he sent Scott-James his address and asked "please send any proofs here".

The significance of this reconstruction is first, that discrepancies between the British and American texts are to be resolved generally

[8] Letter from Michael Horniman of A. P. Watt Ltd. to Richard J. Finneran, 26 September 1979. Mr Horniman confirms that A. P. Watt was not involved in the publication of the poems in question in American periodicals.

I am grateful to Miss Maureen Brown, Assistant to the Editors, for informing me that the files of *The Atlantic Monthly* show that permission fees were paid in care of Scott-James. I would also like to thank Miss Karen Wilcox of *The Nation*, Mr David Seidman of *The New Republic*, and Mr Charles Seaton of *The Spectator* for searching their files for relevant material, even though none was discovered. I have been unable to locate any archives of the *London Mercury*, which may have been lost when that journal was absorbed by *Life and Letters To-day* in May 1939.

[9] The presence in the Scott-James Papers of a corrected carbon typescript of "A Stick of Incense" suggests that Scott-James had been offered that poem but declined to publish it. Had he printed it, the *London Mercury* would have included poems 7–19 of *Last Poems and Two Plays*. Instead, the December 1938 issue includes poems 12–16, the January 1939 issue poems 17–19, and the March 1939 issue poems 7–10.

in favour of the former; and, secondly, that the *London Mercury* texts carry considerable authority — even those in the March 1939 issue, since they were probably printed from copy supplied by Yeats himself.

The variant readings between *Last Poems and Two Plays* and *Last Poems & Plays* comprise the second overriding textual problem in *Last Poems*. We have already discussed in the previous chapter the collaboration between Mrs Yeats and Thomas Mark in 1939 and again in 1949 on *New Poems*, and *Last Poems* was accorded the same treatment. In this instance we have no choice but to examine the textual problems in each poem, drawing on the extant manuscript material. The archive for *Last Poems* is a rich one, including an extensive collection of manuscripts and type-scripts in the National Library of Ireland (MS. 13,593); some manuscripts and typescripts in the collection of Michael B. Yeats; typescripts of two poems in the Scott-James papers at the Human-ities Research Center, University of Texas; the page proofs of *Last Poems and Two Plays* with corrections by Mrs Yeats and F. R. Higgins, in the collection of Michael B. Yeats; and a copy of *Last Poems and Two Plays* with a correction by Mrs Yeats (and the draft table of contents slipped into it), formerly in the collection of Michael B. Yeats.[10] Of the materials cited in the previous chapter, of relevance to *Last Poems* are the three copies of *Last Poems & Plays* with Mrs Yeats's corrections; Mrs Yeats's "Notes on '*A Note on the Texts*'"; and some manuscripts and typescripts from the Edith Shackleton Heald papers at Harvard University.

For the basic texts of "Last Poems" in the new edition of *Poems*, I have followed the English periodical version for those poems published during Yeats's lifetime; and the final typescript for those unpublished at the time of his death. I have accepted a small per-centage of the posthumous emendations made by Mrs Yeats, F. R. Higgins, and Thomas Mark (and possibly others); and I have added one or two new emendations which seem required.

"Under Ben Bulben"

The first poem in the collection offers a paradigm of the problems which we will encounter throughout. One major difficulty is

[10] The copy of *Last Poems and Two Plays* was item #511 in Sotheby's sale in London on 13 May 1980; I have not traced its present whereabouts. A fourth copy of *Last Poems & Plays* in the collection of Anne Yeats includes corrections only to *Purgatory* and *The Death of Cuchulain*.

establishing what is the final typescript in the maze of material in the National Library of Ireland. The typescript has three pages. Of page one (parts I–III of the poem), there is an undated, corrected carbon, with the typed heading "His Convictions"; the original of this is in the Scott-James Papers at the University of Texas. The National Library of Ireland also has two corrected carbons of a lost original: one has "His Convictions" revised to "His Certainties" and is marked "correct Sept 16"; the other has "His Convictions" changed to "Under Benbulben" and is undated. Of page two (part IV), the National Library of Ireland holds an original and a second original with two carbons, all corrected. It is clear that the first original is an early version to which Yeats added punctuation; with those corrections, it is the source of the second original and its carbons. Page two of the poem at the University of Texas was typed after the revision of the latter typescript, although the correction of "perople" to "people" was either overlooked or, more likely, made after the Texas typescript was prepared. Of page three (parts V–VI), the National Library of Ireland has an uncorrected carbon of a lost original, marked "WBY correct Sept 23"; and two carbons of an original at the University of Texas. One, uncorrected, is headed "correct Sept 23"; the other is undated but must be the final version, as it is the only source for the change of "brags of public loss" to "no conventional phrase" (l. 89).[11] By the presence of holes for a paper-fastener in the upper left-hand corner, it is clear that Mrs Yeats considered as the correct version "Under Benbulben" for page one, one of the corrected carbons for page two, and the undated carbon for page three. I have used those three pages for the basic text of the work in the new *Poems*.[12]

A second problem with "Under Ben Bulben" is the matter of the "deathbed revisions". Dorothy Wellesley asserts that on the evening of 26 January 1939, Yeats "was able to give Mrs. Yeats corrections for 'The Death of Cuchulain' and for the poem 'His Convictions' which he changed to 'Under Ben Bulben'" (LDW 195).[13] Unfortunately, Mrs Yeats does not seem to have entered these

---

[11] The date of "September 4, 1938", which first appears in the Cuala edition (it is not on the proofs), is not supported by any evidence on the typescripts.

[12] I believe that this is the same typescript which Jon Stallworthy discusses in *Vision and Revision* (pp. 172–4), explaining that "from its alterations I deduce [it] to be the last" (p. 172).

[13] Cf. Hone, p. 477; and Virginia Moore, *The Unicorn: William Butler Yeats's Search for Reality* (New York: Macmillan, 1954), pp. 441–2.

corrections on to any of the extant typescripts or to have retained a copy of them, despite her usual thoroughness in such matters.[14]

A final area of concern is the source of the newspaper versions of the poem which appeared on 3 February 1939 in the *Irish Times*, the *Irish Independent*, and (ll. 84—94 only) the *Irish Press*. Although it is conceivable that Mrs Yeats prepared a clean typescript and two carbons to submit to the press, the evidence suggests that she prepared only a single new typescript to send to Constantine P. Curran, entrusting him to see to the publication of the work in the Dublin papers. The Curran Collection in University College, Dublin, has a letter to him from Mrs Yeats on 22 February 1939, which begins "I cannot thank you for your very great kindness during the last three weeks". Attached to the letter is a typescript of "Under Ben Bulben" and a clipping of the poem's appearance in the *Irish Independent*. This typescript is very close to what I take to be the final typescript in the National Library of Ireland, the most noticeable difference being the line "And Wilson, Blake and Calvert, Claude" (a misreading of Yeats's correction), which is used in both newspaper editions.[15] It seems clear, then, that the Curran typescript is the source for all the newspaper versions. Moreover, the different emendations to that typescript made by the several newspapers cannot have Yeats's (or even Mrs Yeats's) authority.

[14] A possible exception is the exclamation point which has been added in pencil at l. 26 (it is also found on one earlier typescript). However, since Mrs Yeats's handwriting was not altogether distinct from that of Yeats, it is impossible to say if a change on the order of, say, cancelling a word or adding a comma was done by Yeats or his wife. Infrared or ultraviolet photography of the manuscripts (which I have not attempted) would be of no use except in the very unlikely possibility that they consistently used inks of a significantly different composition, for which there is no evidence. And the problem would still remain as to whether a revision by Mrs Yeats was made at his dictation or after his death. See William H. O'Donnell, "Infrared and Ultraviolet Photography of Manuscripts", *Publications of the Bibliographical Society of America*, 69, No. 4 (Fourth Quarter, 1975), 574—83. Having used the techniques on the manuscripts of Yeats's *The Speckled Bird*, O'Donnell concluded that "it would not be an exaggeration to say that infrared and ultraviolet photography can achieve spectacular results only in sharply limited and, for the most part, unpredictable instances" (p. 576).

[15] On all the typescripts in the National Library of Ireland, the line is typed "Calvert, Palmer, Wilson, Claude" (the earliest version also has a comma after "Claude"). Yeats's correction is not especially clear on the "Under Ben Bulben" typescript, but it is apparent from the two other typescripts that the intended reading is indeed "Calvert and Wilson, Blake and Claude". Moreover, the line is typed that way on the Texas typescript.

I shall discuss first those emendations to the final National Library of Ireland corrected carbon typescript which have been admitted into the new *Poems*:

Title: "Benbulben" has been changed to "Ben Bulben", to accord not only with ll. 11 and 84 but also with the draft table of contents for the volume.

2: "Mariotic" has been corrected to "Mareotic". Mrs Yeats gave this change to Thomas Mark in a letter of 17 April 1939, providing him with the cross-reference to "Demon and Beast"; she also made the revision in her own copy of *Last Poems and Two Plays*. Further, she wrote Mark on 15 April 1939 "that your eagle eye will notice in the second line of 'Under Ben Bulben' (one of the new poems I shall be sending you,) 'Round the Mareotic lake'. That 'c', instead of 'd', was a subject of much discussion between WB and myself, he wanted it for sound, and I finally discovered a respectable authority for it!"[16]

4: "set all the cocks a-crow" has been emended to "set the cocks a-crow". On the several typescripts, the line was typed as "When they set the cocks a-crow" or "When that set the cocks a-crow" (obviously a typing error). Yeats revised this to "Spoke and set all the cocks a-crow" on three of the four typescripts, including that headed "Under Benbulben". However, he cancelled "all" on the "His Certainties" typescript, and the word does not appear in the Curran typescript, the Cuala proofs, or any of the printed editions. The deletion, which clearly improves the rhythm of the line, is very likely a "deathbed revision", recalled by Mrs Yeats when she was preparing the Curran typescript.[17]

45: I have emended to Yeats's preferred form, "Michael Angelo", which seems absolutely required in "Long-legged Fly" (l. 26) and is consistent with "Michael Robartes and the Dancer" (l. 32). Yeats inherited the two-word form from, among others, William Blake and John Butler Yeats.

85: I have corrected and emended "Druncliffe" to "Drumcliff".

---

[16] Her authority may well have been Anthony De Cosson, *Mareotis: Being a Short Account of the History and Ancient Monuments of the North-Western Desert of Egypt and of Lake Mareotis* (London: Country Life, 1935), e.g. "Mareotic soil" (p. 41). Alternatively, the *Encyclopedia Britannica*, 11th ed. (1910), IX, 22, refers to "Mareotic wine".

[17] Without the benefit of the Curran typescript, Stallworthy also concluded that the deletion of "all" was a "deathbed revision" (*Vision and Revision*, p. 174).

Mrs Yeats included the emendation in the list sent to Mark on 14 June 1939: "as in Celtic Twilight etc. It is the old spelling". The reference is to the story "Drumcliff and Rosses".

I do not think it is necessary here to discuss all of the emendations which "Under Ben Bulben" suffered after Yeats's death — first at the hands of the newspaper editors and/or compositors and later by Mrs Yeats and Mark in *Last Poems and Two Plays*, *Last Poems & Plays* and the 1949 *Poems* (those interested in that process can of course retrace it in the *Variorum Poems*). I suspect that many readers will feel that the text in the new *Poems* is insufficiently emended, especially in terms of punctuation. On that problem in general, I can only restate my position as argued in the previous chapter: that Yeats used what Curtis Bradford has termed "rhetorical as opposed to grammatical punctuation"[18] and that he ought to be allowed his preference. With "Under Ben Bulben" in particular, it is clear that most of the additional punctuation was done in the office of the *Irish Independent*: for example, the new commas at the end of ll. 14, 15, 25, 29, 56, and 57 appear in the *Irish Independent* but not in the *Irish Times*, and they are lacking on the Curran typescript. Further, only those at ll. 14 and 15 have any manuscript support, being found on the "His Certainties" typescript and the version presented by Dorothy Wellesley (LDW 185).

As a summary example of how "Under Ben Bulben" was emended, we might examine the opening of the second stanza. The final National Library of Ireland typescript, the Curran typescript, and the *Irish Independent* are identical:

> Swear by those horsemen, by those women,
> Complexion and form prove superhuman,
> That pale, long visaged company
> That airs an immortality
> Completeness of their passions won; . . . .

The comma after "women" also appeared in the *Irish Times*, and it survived through the Cuala proofs and the Cuala volume; but it was deleted in the Macmillan edition. By removing the comma, the following line can apply only to the "women"; but Yeats surely intended it to describe both the "horsemen" and the "women".

---

[18] See *Yeats at Work*, p. 14.

The only support for the deletion of the comma would be the "His Convictions" and the Texas typescripts, but those also lack the comma after "superhuman". Of perhaps greater interest, though, is "airs an immortality". In the *Irish Times* the line reads "airs in immortality"; that reading was carried over into the Cuala proofs and the published volume. In *Last Poems & Plays* the line was changed to "air in immortality". But all three typescripts in the National Library of Ireland, the Texas typescript, the Curran typescript, and the text given by Wellesley (LDW 185) read "airs an immortality", and that seems to me indisputably the superior version.[19] "Completeness of their passion won", the horsemen and the women are enabled, as the OED puts it, "to wear openly, expose to public view" their immortality. Yeats's poems are filled with references to "air" as a noun, but "Under Ben Bulben" is the only instance in which he uses it as a verb. I suspect that he took a special pleasure in the new use of "air", one he had discovered as early as "the first complete, but rough, verse draft".[20]

"Three Songs to the One Burden"

The text in the new *Poems* has been taken from the corrected carbon typescript in the National Library of Ireland. A few necessary emendations have been made:

I, 10: On an earlier typescript Yeats had changed "Mannion" to "Maughan". On the final typescript he reverted to "Mannion" and revised l. 2, but he did not make the required change in l. 10.

I, 10: I have emended "Mananaan" to "Manannan", the spelling in "The Wanderings of Oisin" since 1912 and in Yeats's major sources, such as Lady Gregory's *Cuchulain of Muirthemne* and H. d'Arbois de Jubainville's *The Irish Mythological Cycle*.

III, 23: I have corrected "whats" to "what's".

III, 25: The single quotation mark at the beginning of the line has been deleted. In an earlier version of this passage, Yeats had

---

[19] In *Vision and Revision* (p. 174), Stallworthy suggests that "air in immortality" might be another "deathbed revision", but that seems unlikely in view of the reading on the Curran typescript.

[20] *Vision and Revision*, pp. 160–1.

used a direct quotation; and when he wrote out the final version (see below) he may have included the quotation mark before deciding to modify the lines to indirect discourse.

The fact that the refrains are set off from the stanzas on the last typescript may well be a remnant of the poem having been a dialogue between a "Singer" and a "Speaker" in the earlier drafts, but I have let the spaces stand.

The most interesting differences between the final typescript and the published texts concern two places where Yeats's corrections have been misread. Both occur in the third part of the poem. On the last typescript, l. 16 read "An admired, a brilliant figure". With a single line, Yeats crossed out "An admired, a" and indicated in the margin "A famous / ——". I take it that Yeats intended "A famous" to be followed by what was not cancelled. As the cancellation line does not go through the comma, the proper reading would therefore be "A famous, brilliant figure" rather than "A famous, a brilliant figure", as in all published texts.

The other error occurred in l. 23. Yeats had cancelled ll. 23–6 of the last typescript and written out the following revision:

> And no one knows whats yet to come.
> For Patrick Pearse had said
> 'That in every generation
> Must Ireland's blood be shed.

This was misread to create the awkward line "And yet who knows what's yet to come". In the *Spectator* and the Cuala edition, the line was followed by a comma; this was changed to a question mark in *Last Poems & Plays*. I am in fact uncertain about the period which appears in the new *Poems*: there is a period some distance below the line, and it is difficult to tell if it belongs to that line or to an earlier cancelled passage. But it is hardly a comma and certainly not a question mark.

"The Black Tower"

The text in the new *Poems* is taken from the carbon typescript in the collection of Michael B. Yeats. The original of this is apparently lost. The carbon has "January 21 1939" added in original typewriter, probably an addition by Mrs Yeats after Yeats's death. Two other original typescripts survive, one in the collection of Michael B. Yeats and the other in the National Library of Ireland. I have admitted two emendations:

21: "The tower's old cook must climb and clamber" has been revised to "The tower's old cook that must climb and clamber". Yeats added "that" to the original typescript in Michael B. Yeats's collection but neglected, I think, to do so on the final carbon typescript. The sentence structure and punctuation of the passage had given Yeats trouble. On the National Library of Ireland typescript he had tried the following:

> The tower's old cook must climb and clamber
> Catching small birds in the dew of the morn.
> When we hale men lie stretched in slumber;
> Swears that he hears the great king's horn.

date: the comma after "21" has been included.

The Cuala proofs are quite close to the corrected carbon. Most of the additional punctuation found in *Last Poems and Two Plays* and the other later volumes has no support in any of the typescripts. It is of course possible to argue for the heavier and regularised punctuation of the refrains in the Macmillan edition. But if the refrains are indeed meant to produce, as Daniel A. Harris has suggested, "a strange, eerie resonance", their unorthodox elements may be purposeful.[21]

"Cuchulain Comforted"

The new *Poems* text is based on the carbon typescript in the collection of Michael B. Yeats. The original of this carbon appears to be lost. The carbon is uncorrected except for the addition by Yeats of the "e" in "Comforted" in the title, a correction of a typing error. The carbon is dated "January 13 1939". In the National Library of Ireland there is a corrected original typescript and a corrected carbon of that typescript; on both Yeats has changed the title from "Cuchullain Dead" to "Cuchullain Comforted". I have admitted the following emendations into the basic text:

---

[21] *Yeats: Coole Park & Ballylee*, p. 248.

Title: Yeats's spelling has been regularised to the form he had preferred since 1904, "Cuchulain".

3: the typing error "[space]yes" for "Eyes" has been corrected.

7: the capital on "Shroud", found on the National Library of Ireland typescripts, has been added to conform with "Shrouds" in l. 3.

12, 13, 16, 19, 22: the initial quotation marks have been added (some of these are included on the National Library of Ireland typescripts).

13: the semi-colon, which has been added in pencil on the National Library of Ireland original typescript, has been included.

16: the missing apostrophe in "needles" has been supplied.

17: the exclamation point after "do!" has been emended to a period followed by a single quotation. I believe this was a typing error, as an exclamation point does not seem in accord with the tone of "Cuchulain Comforted". The other typescripts have a double quotation mark typed over a period; the manuscript has a double quotation mark but is unpunctuated.

date: the comma after "13" has been supplied.

The carbon in Michael B. Yeats's collection, which was itself based on the carbon in the National Library of Ireland, must have been used as the copy for the Cuala proofs — as can be seen in the misprint of "Yes" in l. 3 of the proofs. However, for reasons which remain unclear to me, in revising the proofs Mrs Yeats decided to adopt two substantive revisions which Yeats had tried on the original typescript in the National Library of Ireland but which he apparently decided against carrying over to the final carbon typescript. Thus she used "Now must we sing" instead of "Now we shall sing" (l. 19) and "had nor human tunes nor words" instead of "had nor human notes nor words" (l. 23). In the first instance, the result was to introduce a single example of inverted word order into the poem, reduce the alliterative values of the line, and indeed modify Yeats's depiction of the Shrouds — now somehow forced to sing (by "ancient rule"?) rather than choosing to do so. In the second change, the interlocking rime on "notes"/"throats", which is surely an intentional doubling at the conclusion of a terza rima lyric ("notes nor words"/"throats of birds"), is lost. Moreover, in the proper text the spectral nature of the Shrouds is enhanced by their lack not simply of human melodies but indeed of human sounds.

"Three Marching Songs"

The text in the new *Poems* follows the final corrected original typescript in the National Library of Ireland. The following emendations have been admitted:

I, 20, 30: Yeats revised "All that's finished" at l. 10 to read
"All that is finished", but he failed to make the same change in
ll. 20 and 30. I have made the emendation on the assumption
that in "Three Marching Songs" he intended the refrains to be
identical.

II, 17, 27: as in the previous instance, Yeats changed "down
the mountain pass" to "through the mountain pass" in l. 7 but
not in ll. 17 and 27. Again, I believe that he intended regular
refrains.

II, 18: I have added the comma after "son," also to keep the
refrains identical.

II, 21: I have corrected "theres" to "there's".

II, note: Yeats's note reads "'Airy' may be an old pronunciation of eary[.] I often heard it in Galway & Sligo". In the Cuala
edition, this was printed as "'Airy' may be an old pronunciation of 'eerie' often heard in Galway and Sligo". I have emended
"eary" to "eerie" and have added the quotation marks around it
and the period after it, but in all other respects Yeats's wording
is followed.

The fact that no emendations are required in the third part of
the poem brings us to one of the interesting textual problems in
"Three Marching Songs". That is, the Cuala proofs as well as the
published edition suggest that there was a later typescript of part
III which was lost after *Last Poems and Two Plays* was published;
and that when the Macmillan edition was printed, the National
Library of Ireland typescript was the latest one available. Folios
I–K in National Library of Ireland MS. 13,593 (35) have the poem
in the order 3–1–2, as in "Three Songs to the Same Tune" in *A
Full Moon in March*. Folio I is headed "Three Marching Songs (To
the Tune of 'O'Donnell Abu")". Folios J and K were then revised:
folio J on folio L, and folio K on folios M–N. These revised versions
were prepared with a different typewriter. It is of course possible
that Yeats did not ask for a new typescript of folio I because he was
happy with that part of the poem as it stood; however, the title on

the top has not been changed, nor has "I" been corrected to "III". And on the revised typescripts (folios L–N), "I" was first "II", "II" first "III". It thus seems almost certain that what eventually became the third part of "Three Marching Songs" was also retyped and that that missing typescript was the source of the text in the Cuala edition. I list below the variants from the Cuala proofs, excluding those which were probably typographical errors:

III, 7, 27: there was no comma after "tambourine", although the comma is found at l. 17.

III, 12: there was no comma in "Money I had and it went in the night".

III, 13: there was no comma in "Strong drink I had and it brought me to sorrow".

III, 15: "tune" is followed by a comma rather than a colon.

These readings (as well as two other variants which I do not believe Yeats was responsible for) carry over into the printed edition of *Last Poems and Two Plays*; in *Last Poems & Plays*, though, the poem was revised to follow exactly folio I. In the new *Poems* I have been tempted to emend part III of "Three Marching Songs" as suggested by the above list. But in the final analysis I have chosen in favour of the certain evidence of an extant typescript rather than the hypothetical readings of one that I have been unable to discover.

The second interesting textual problem in the poem concerns what has been a serious error in ll. 13–14 of Part II. The final typescript originally read as follows:

> Nor were we born in the peasant's cot
> Where man forgives if the belly gain.

Yeats changed "in the peasant's cot" to "under the thatch" but then decided to revert to the typed version. He also crossed out "we" and wrote "not" above it; he crossed out "Nor" and wrote above it what could be taken either as "We" or as "were". In *Last Poems and Two Plays* the revision was read correctly, but an unsupported change was introduced in the following line:

> We were not born in the peasant's cot
> Where men forgive if the belly gain.

However, the worst change was still to come. For the Macmillan edition, someone (I suspect Mark) apparently misread the correction on the typescript, assuming (a) that the word written above the cancelled "Nor" was "Were"; (b) that Yeats intended to cancel the typed "were" but forgot to do so; and (c) that Yeats did not intend to cancel the typed "we". And, of course, the period was replaced by a question mark. We are thus given

> Were we not born in the peasant's cot
> Where men forgive if the belly gain?

The revision may make the speaker of the poem more democratic, but it hardly accords with his hierarchical beliefs: even if he *had* been born in such a setting, he would scarcely have boasted of that fact. Moreover, the text of *Last Poems & Plays* makes the following lines senseless:

> More dread the life that we live,
> How can the mind forgive?

Yeats wants to contrast those who live only in the "belly" and are thus blissfully unaware of the state of the modern world, with those who, like the speaker, live in the "mind" and thereby understand and "dread" the coming dissolution.

That Yeats clearly intended the reading used in the new edition of *Poems* is suggested by two earlier manuscript versions of the lines in question:

> Nor were we born in the peasants cot
> Where man forgives if his belly gain

and

> Nor were we born of a peasant cot
> Where man gives, if his belly gain[.]

The note in the Macmillan edition that the poems were "Rewritten December 1938", heretofore ascribed to Yeats (as in VP 613), would have been the work of Mrs Yeats.

"In Tara's Halls"

The text in the new *Poems* is based on the corrected original typescript in the National Library. One emendation has been admitted:

12: the typographical error of "haroow" for "harrow" has been corrected.

The National Library of Ireland also has a corrected carbon of the same typescript. It seems clear that the carbon was corrected first, the revisions that Yeats wished to retain transferred to the original, and further changes then made on the original. The Cuala proofs appear to have been printed from the original typescript, with the usual increase in punctuation and what I suspect was the accidental omission of "that" (l. 7). However, in the process of proofreading two variants from the carbon were adopted: "king" (l. 10) and "women" (l. 15), the readings of both the original typescript and the proofs, were replaced by "man" and "woman".

In fact, Yeats had had some difficulty with ll. 14–15. The typed version was

'God I have loved, the time to die will come
When my heart asks to have its love returned.'

On the carbon he tried

'God I have loved, but should I ask return
From God or woman the time were come to die.'

The last version was reached on the original typescript:

'God I have loved, but should I ask return
Of God or women, the time were come to die.'

"The Statues"

The text in the new *Poems* is based on the corrected original typescript in the National Library of Ireland.[22] This is headed "Final version Sept 23" at the top and "correct Sept 23" at the bottom. I have admitted one emendation:

25: "Cuchullain" has been regularised to Yeats's preferred "Cuchulain", as was done in "Cuchulain Comforted".

---

[22] Stallworthy's discussion of "The Statues" (*Vision and Revision*, pp. 123–43) does not draw on this typescript or on a draft of the second stanza of the poem which is included with the manuscripts of "Politics" (National Library of Ireland MS. 13,593 (48), folio B). Stallworthy also does not take into account the Heald typescript.

The most complex question about the text of "The Statues" involves an emendation which I did not make but which many readers will doubtless feel is required: the elimination of the punctuation in "formless, spawning, fury wrecked" (l. 30). The early typescripts of the poem, including the one sent to Edith Shackleton Heald on 28 June 1938 (L 911), have the line unpunctuated. Dorothy Wellesley's copy, presumably a carbon of Heald's, adds (if we assume her transcription to be accurate) the comma after "formless" (LDW 167). Two commas appear for the first time on the penultimate typescript in the National Library of Ireland. In *The Nation* (15 April 1939) the line reads "formless, spawning fury wrecked"; but in the *London Mercury* (March 1939) and the Cuala proofs the punctuation follows exactly the final typescript. However, F. R. Higgins made a note on the proofs of "punctuation trouble". The solution which he and Mrs Yeats came up with for *Last Poems and Two Plays* is, I think, the worst possible one: "formless spawning, fury wrecked". In *Last Poems & Plays* the unpunctuated version is used.

Mrs Yeats later commented on the problem in her "Notes on '*A Note on the Texts*'":

> *Statues* corrected by WBY − see Macmillan ed: the comma in Mercury & Cuala is incorrect. The line reads "And by its formless spawning fury wrecked" (we Irish . . . wrecked by its formless spawning fury)[.]

The key phrase is of course "corrected by WBY". I have found no evidence of Yeats having made such a revision, and clearly Mrs Yeats was unaware of any as late as the final correction of proofs for *Last Poems and Two Plays*. It seems almost certain that Thomas Mark suggested the change when he was checking the proofs of the second volume of the Coole Edition *Poems* in 1939 and that Mrs Yeats silently assented.

In my opinion, "formless, spawning, fury wrecked" is so seminal an instance of Yeats's rhetorical punctuation that it might be allowed to stand, despite its being "incorrect" (surely grammarians would follow *The Nation* and Dorothy Wellesley's typescript and prefer "formless, spawning fury wrecked"?). I think that Yeats was trying to accomplish two things with his punctuation of the last two typescripts. First, his version slows down the reading of the line; thus, after a series of quite heavy accents, the heaviest of all falls on "wrecked", emphasising the brilliant rime with "intellect" and "sect". Secondly, Yeats's punctuation gives "formless" and "spawning" not merely adjectival values but almost nominal force: the "modern tide" is characterised not simply by a "fury", however modified, but by formlessness *and* spawning *and* fury.

A minor problem about "The Statues" is the date of "April 9th. 1938", which first appears in the Cuala edition (it is lacking on the proofs). This appears to be an error for the date of "Long-legged Fly", which Yeats told Dorothy Wellesley on 4 April 1938 was "finished, though I have not yet made a clean copy" and which he sent to her on 11 April 1938 (LDW 160–1).[23] Yeats told Wellesley that he had not finished "The Statues" until 10 June 1938 (LDW 164).

"News for the Delphic Oracle"

The text in the new *Poems* is taken from the corrected carbon typescript in the National Library of Ireland. No emendations have been required.

This typescript is identical to the version in the *London Mercury* (March 1939) except that on the typescript "Pelius" has been corrected to "Peleus". The correction is in pencil and was probably made by Mrs Yeats for *Last Poems & Plays*, as both *The New Republic* (22 March 1939) and *Last Poems and Two Plays* also reproduce the error. In her "Notes on '*A Note on the Texts*'", Mrs Yeats stated that Peleus "was corrected"; she also remarked that "wade" for "wades" in the Cuala edition was indeed a misprint, as "Yeats wanted the 's' sound there".

"Long-legged Fly"

The text in the new *Poems* is taken from the final original typescript in the National Library of Ireland. One emendation has been admitted:

> 17: I have regularised "Practice" to "Practise", as in "Shepherd and Goatherd" and elsewhere.[24]

[23] In a radio broadcast quoted in *Vision and Revision* (p. 115), Edith Shackleton Heald recalls Yeats working on "Long-legged Fly" at the home of Dorothy Wellesley. Wellesley herself notes that "Yeats came to Penns on March 24th [1938] for a week. He was full of creative energy, but tired easily" (LDW 160). I know of no evidence to support Richard Ellmann's dating of "Long-legged Fly" as "Nov. 1937" in *The Identity of Yeats*, 2nd ed. (London: Faber, 1964), p. 294, which seems unlikely.

[24] VP 617 offers "Practice" – a spelling found only in *The Nation* – and overlooks the variants, "Practise" being the reading in all texts published from 1939–49.

I suspect that some readers will prefer the comma at the end of the first line, which did not appear until the Cuala edition. That Yeats did not require it is confirmed by its absence from not only the final typescript but also the *London Mercury* (March 1939), *The Nation* (15 April 1939), the Cuala proofs, and the typescripts given to Dorothy Wellesley (LDW 161) and Edith Shackleton Heald. The reading "a street" for "the street" (l. 18) is likewise absent from all those versions except the Cuala proofs. Finally, as I think it is at least possible that Yeats discriminated between italicised and non-italicised refrains, here and elsewhere in the new *Poems* I have not regularised but have followed the final version. In "Long-legged Fly", it is certain that the refrains should be separated by a space, as was done in all editions until the Macmillan volume.

"A Bronze Head"

The text in the new *Poems* is taken from the corrected carbon typescript in the National Library of Ireland. This is dated "correct August 12". I have admitted the following emendations:

7: I have corrected "Hysterico-passio" to "*Hysterica-passio*".
26: I have regularised "stye" to "sty", as in "Crazy Jane Talks with the Bishop".[25]
27: I have regularised "revery" to "reverie", as in "Meditations in Time of Civil War" and elsewhere.

"A Bronze Head" offers perhaps the most complex textual problems of any poem in Yeats's canon. The final carbon typescript is corrected both in ink by Yeats and in pencil by, I think, Mrs Yeats. Furthermore, I believe that the pencil corrections were made after his death and without his authority, and thus I have accepted only the correction to "*Hysterica-passio*". The accompanying chart shows the variants in the poem based on the following texts. *TS1*: the corrected carbon typescript before the pencil revisions; *LM*: the *London Mercury* (March 1939); *NR*: *The New Republic* (22 March 1939); *TS2*: the typescript after the pencil corrections; *Proofs*: the Cuala proofs; *LPTP*: *Last Poems and Two Plays*; *LLP*: *Last Poems & Plays*. The crucial pencil

[25] VP 619 overlooks the spelling "stye" in the *London Mercury*.

Variants in "A Bronze Head"

	TS1	LM	NR	TS2	Proofs	LPTP	LPP
2	super-human	super-human	superhuman	superhuman	super-human	super-human	superhuman
4	sky;	sky;	sky;	sky;	sky;	sky	sky
5	die;)	die;)	die)	die;)	die;)	die)	die:)
7	Hysterico-	Hysterico-	Hysterico-	Hysterica-	Hysterico-	Hysterico-	*Hysterica-*
9	light	light	light	light	light	light	light,
10	woman's	woman	woman	woman	woman	woman	woman
11	right	right,	right,	right?	right,	right?	right?
12	may be	may be	maybe	may be	may be	may be	maybe
14	hold	hold	hold	held	held	held	held
15	starting post	starting-post	starting-post	starting post	starting-post	starting-post	starting-post
20	itself.	itself.	itself.	itself;	itself.	itself;	itself;
21	my	my	my	my	my	my	My
21	child.	child!	child!	child.	child!	child!	child!
22	supernatural;	supernatural;	supernatural;	supernatural;	supernatural,	supernatural,	supernatural;
24	fall,	fall;	fall;	fall	fall;	fall;	fall;
26	stye	stye	sty	stye	stye	sty	sty
27	revery	revery	revery	revery	revery	reverie	reverie
27	knave	knave,	knave,	knave	knave,	knave,	knave

corrections are those to ll. 2, 7, 10, 11, and 14. What is important is that the pencil corrections do not seem to have been available when the periodical typescripts were prepared, when the Cuala proofs were printed, and probably not even when those proofs were corrected. It is not until the 1940 Macmillan edition that all of the corrections appear in print. If, for example, both periodicals had received a typescript reading "A mouthful held the extreme of life and death", it is unlikely that they both would have misprinted "hold". Likewise, the compositors at the Cuala Press are not likely to have added a hyphen in "superhuman", misspelled "Hysterica", and overlooked the question mark after "right?"

My conjecture, then, is that Mrs Yeats added the pencil corrections in the process of checking the poem for the Macmillan edition. However, it must be admitted that she was adamant that *Last Poems & Plays* offered the proper text. "A Bronze Head" appears twice on her "Notes on '*A Note on the Texts*'": she indicates "corrected in Macmillan ed." on the first page and "this *is* correct in Cuala 'Last Poems' ("held" not *hold*)" on the second page. Moreover, in April 1949 Thomas Mark had queried the text of the poem, as follows:

'A Bronze Head', v. 2, last lines

> 'in a breath
> A mouthful held . . .'

I have not read McTaggart, and I probably miss the meaning. I suppose it should not read

> 'a breath,
> A mouthful, held . . . [.]'

Mrs Yeats's response on 29 April 1949 is worth quoting at length:

I don[']t think there should be a comma after 'a breath'. I think the idea is of a sudden breathlessness, an intake of breath which comes with the sudden vision of great beauty or great nobility. − (and in a breath a mouthful held the extreme of life and death). 'Profound McTaggart refers back to

> 'Or maybe substance can be composite'

and the lines

' . . . and in a breath
A mouthful held the extreme of life & death'

refer back to

'No dark tomb-haunter once; her form all full
As though with magnanimity of light.'

(expressed in last line as 'extreme of life and death'). In another
sense the 'breath' refers to the complete person.

This is a useful comment, but it fails to address the question of
the complexity of tenses, both in "A Bronze Head" as a whole and
in the second stanza in particular. The poem is written so as to
make it extraordinarily difficult to determine − as long as we stay
within the poem itself − whether its subject is alive or dead. As Jon
Stallworthy has perceptively remarked, the work depicts someone
who is "alive and dead, and alive-in-death".[26] The poem begins
simply enough, in present time (the echo of the opening of Brown-
ing's "My Last Duchess" is surely not accidental). But the vision of
the vibrant eyes amidst the "withered and mummy-dead" bust
leads the speaker to conceive of the woman as both "human" and
"super-human". He then speculates on the kind of existence she
will have after death: the only suggestion that she might not
already be dead is "die" rather than "died", but it is an ambiguous
one.

The second stanza begins in the past: "No dark tomb-haunter
once". The next two lines accomplish the feat of making the past
seem present and alive, by the simple but brilliant device of omitting
any verb. "Who can tell / Which of her forms has shown her substance right" returns to the present time, but the "forms" encompass
the past (ll. 8−10), the present (ll. 1−3), and, perhaps ("has" rather
than "had" is the clue), the future (ll. 4−7).[27] But rather than rest
with that question or attempt to answer it, the speaker rushes on to
suggest, following "Profound McTaggart", that no single form can
ever express the full identity of an individual. Since McTaggart had

---

[26] *Between the Lines*, p. 221. In a dogmatically New Critical reading in *W. B.
Yeats, The Tragic Phase: A Study of the Last Poems* (London: Routledge &
Kegan Paul, 1951), p. 80, Vivienne Koch has no doubts: "the bronze head is
the head of someone no longer alive".

[27] The triple pun on "forms" − outside appearances, moulds for the plaster bust,
and Platonic Forms − is one of Yeats's most ingenious.

died in 1925, his "thought" is presented in the past tense; but I would suggest that Yeats wants to offer the philosophical principle that "substance can be composite", as exemplified in the statement that a single breath can "hold the extreme of life and death", as a concept valid in the present, applicable to all forms in which the woman has been, or will be, embodied. Having established that principle, the speaker is then free to select which forms of the subject he will choose to memorialise in the final two stanzas of the poem — where, as Stallworthy notes, "I" first appears.[28] In sum, then, I argue for the superiority of "hold" rather than "held" for two reasons: it continues the ambiguity about the subject's current state found in "die" and "has"; and it widens the frame of reference for the concept that "substance can be composite".[29]

[28] *Between the Lines*, p. 221: "only in stanzas III and IV does the commentator appear".

[29] Our understanding of the philosophical concept in this difficult second stanza has not been much advanced by previous commentators. Koch, for example, suggests that we need not bother about McTaggart's ideas and that "the introduction of his commonplace name [?] into the body of this most 'rich, dark' poem is a masterstroke of strategy. It is a spike of everydayness which relieves the sombre decor and confers a kind of daylight sensibleness on the inquiry" (*W. B. Yeats, The Tragic Phase*, p. 82). In *A Commentary on the Collected Poems of W. B. Yeats* (Stanford: Stanford University Press, 1968), p. 499, A. Norman Jeffares glosses "Profound McTaggart" with a quite irrelevant passage from McTaggart's *Human Immortality and Pre-existence*.

It seems clear that Yeats's primary source was the first volume of *The Nature of Existence* (Cambridge: University Press, 1921), a copy of which is preserved in his library. Much of this volume is devoted to the concept of "substance". McTaggart's term is not "composite" but "compound", and he attempts to demonstrate that "there can be no simple substance" (p. 179). Yeats's direct source may have been the conclusion to the chapter entitled "Compound Substances", where McTaggart takes up some possible objections to his argument that "all substances are compound" (p. 138):

Or again, the objection may be made, not that the compound substance is too unimportant, as compared with its parts, to be a substance, but that it is too important, as compared with its parts, to be taken as compounded of them. If a man, for example, is regarded as standing to his successive states in time as a whole to its parts, and if all the content of man falls in time, he must be considered, not only as a substance, but as a substance compounded of his states in time, which must also be considered as substances. And it may be said that this is unreasonable. For, even on the assumption that the whole content of the man falls in time, there is much in the nature of the man which is not to be found in any of his states. How then can he be compounded of the states? *cont'd overleaf*

The other crucial textual problem in "A Bronze Head" is the proper reading in l. 10, "woman's" or "woman". Here it seems clear that Yeats wants to *contrast* the "gentle" outward appearance of the woman with her inner "magnanimity of light", taking "magnanimity" primarily in the sense of "loftiness of thought or purpose; grandeur of designs, nobly ambitious spirit" as well as "nobility of feeling; superiority to petty resentment or jealousy; generous disregard of injuries" (OED; cf. "The strength that gives our blood and state magnanimity of its own desire" in "Blood and the Moon"). It is thus difficult to associate magnanimity with gentleness, and certainly the description in the third stanza emphasises the woman's "wildness". Moreover, by this point in the poem the speaker realises that such a simple description as "a most gentle woman" can never be true to the complexities of identity.

Further support for the reading "a most gentle woman's" can be found if we recall that "A Bronze Head" began as a response to the bronze-painted plaster bust of Maud Gonne in the Municipal Gallery of Modern Art in Dublin.[30] To Yeats, Maud was an image of

> The answer here is that a substance which is made up of substances, and is therefore a group, must have many qualities which are not found in any of its parts (among others, the quality of being the whole, of which they are the parts) and that among these qualities may be some of the greatest importance. For example, France is made up of individual Frenchmen. There is no content in the substance France which does not fall within this, that, or the other Frenchman. Yet France is a nation, and a republic, and no Frenchman is either. And, in the same way, there might be no content in John Smith which did not fall within this, that, or the other of his states in time, and yet he would have many qualities which were not qualities of any of those states, and it might well be that among them were those of his qualities which were of most importance both to himself and to his friends. (p. 142)

[30] Hone, p. 470; there is a black-and-white photograph of the bust on the facing page. "A Bronze Head" may have grown out of Maud's last visit to Yeats, which Hone dates in "the late summer of 1938". There had been little contact between Yeats and Maud for some time, but in the spring of 1938 she wrote to ask permission to quote his poems in her *A Servant of the Queen*. Yeats replied on 16 June 1938, regretting that he had not asked Maud to dine with him in April 1938 (L 909–10). Yeats returned to Dublin sometime between 29 July 1938 (LDW 182) and the first production of *Purgatory* on 10 August 1938. Maud recalled the final meeting in her essay on "Yeats and Ireland", in *Scattering Branches: Tributes to the Memory of W. B. Yeats* (London: Macmillan, 1940), pp. 15–33: "the last time I saw Willie at Riversdale just before he left Ireland for the last time, as we said goodbye, he, sitting in his arm-chair from which he could rise only with great effort, said, 'Maud, we should have gone on with our Castle of the Heroes, we might still do it'" (p. 25).   *cont'd opposite*

"Pallas Athena in that straight back and arrogant head" ("Beautiful Lofty Things"), not "a most gentle woman".

The final difficulty with "A Bronze Head" is, as usual in the poems not published in Yeats's lifetime, the punctuation. Many readers will doubtless prefer the version in *Last Poems & Plays*, though it is curious that Mrs Yeats and/or Mark restored the semi-colon inside the parenthesis in l. 5. However, Yeats did mark the revised typescript "correct", and it may well be that he felt the unorthodox punctuation suitable for an interior monologue at once personal and philosophical, especially one written in the strict rime royal form.

"A Stick of Incense"

The text in the new *Poems* is taken from the corrected carbon typescript in the Scott-James papers at the Humanities Research Center, University of Texas. One emendation has been admitted:

4: the typing error "like" has been corrected to "liked", as on the corrected holograph manuscript in the National Library of Ireland.

There is no support for the question mark at the end of the first line, which was introduced after the printing of the proofs for the Cuala edition.

"Hound Voice"

The text in the new *Poems* is taken from the *London Mercury* for December 1938. One emendation has been admitted:

To thus describe the genesis of "A Bronze Head" is not to insist that the lyric is necessarily "about" Maud or "about" Laurence Campbell's plaster bust. The poem itself of course names neither. It is possible that if Yeats had lived to see what I conjecture would have been called *Under Ben Bulben* through the press, he might have added a note indicating the source of the poem. But that is simply speculation. We are so used to biographical criticism of Yeats that it is difficult to remember that Maud is named but once in all of Yeats's poems (in "Beautiful Lofty Things"). For an example of biographical criticism carried to its *reductio ad absurdum*, witness Jeffares's gloss on "No dark tomb-haunter": "the phrase may derive from Madame MacBride's habit of wearing black flowing garments and a veil, as well as of visiting graveyards on political occasions" (*Commentary*, p. 499).

9: "Hound Voices" has been changed to "Hound voices" to conform not only with l. 7 but also with the three typescripts (an original and carbon, and another original) in the National Library of Ireland and the typescript given to Edith Shackleton Heald.

There is no support for the Cuala edition reading of l. 9 as "Then stumbling to the kill" rather than "That stumbling to the kill". The correct version, a revision of the final corrected carbon typescript (marked "correct Sept 23"), appeared on the proofs but was inexplicably changed before publication.

"John Kinsella's Lament for Mrs. Mary Moore"

In the new *Poems*, the text of the first two parts of the work is based on the *London Mercury* for December 1938, as emended by Yeats in an unpublished letter to F. R. Higgins on 22 November [1938], now at the Humanities Research Center, University of Texas. The text for part III of the poem is based on the version supplied in the letter to Higgins, with some emendations admitted and with some of the punctuation from the *London Mercury* text. I shall first discuss the authority of the *London Mercury* version before considering Yeats's letter to Higgins.

"John Kinsella's Lament for Mrs. Mary Moore" offers a good example of the textual problems in the poems that were published in periodicals before Yeats's death. The copy submitted to the *London Mercury*, doubtless a corrected carbon, is not known to have survived. The *London Mercury* text is identical to the final corrected original typescript in the National Library of Ireland — to which Yeats had added the punctuation — except for the following:

Title: the typescript lacks the period in "Mrs".
2: the typescript lacks the comma.
6: the typescript lacks the comma.
12: the typescript uses a period rather than a question mark.
14: the typescript lacks the capital on "Jew".
14: the typescript lacks the comma.
17: the typescript has a comma after "stories", which is missing not only in the *London Mercury* but also in *The New Republic*,

the Cuala proofs, the Cuala edition, and Dorothy Wellesley's version (LDW 183).

There are three possible explanations for the above variants: (1) misprints by the *London Mercury*; (2) changes made by Yeats when he prepared the typescript for the journal but which he neglected to copy on to the surviving final typescript; and (3) revisions made by Yeats when he read proofs for the journal.[31] Barring the unlikely recovery of the copy used by the *London Mercury* or the proofs, it is impossible to be certain of the correct explanation. My policy in the new *Poems* has been to give a text which appeared in Yeats's lifetime substantial authority and to emend it only when it seems absolutely necessary. In the instance of "John Kinsella's Lament for Mrs. Mary Moore", I suspect that most readers will agree that the *London Mercury* provides a better text than the corrected typescript in the National Library of Ireland, with the possible exception of the lack of a comma after "stories" (l. 17). However, I suspect that many of those same readers will also feel that additional commas are required at ll. 5, 19, 29, and 30 (that at l. 30 is found in Yeats's letter to Higgins, as we shall see). But those commas are in fact lacking on the corrected typescript and in the *London Mercury*, *The New Republic*, and the Cuala proofs.[32] Two of those commas first appear in *Last Poems and Two Plays*, the other two in *Last Poems & Plays*.

It is likely, then, that Yeats's punctuation followed his sense of the rhythm of the poem rather than the rules of grammar. The presence or absence of the commas does not essentially modify the "meaning" of the poem, and readers are of course free to accept the changes made by Mrs Yeats and Thomas Mark. But they should be aware that by doing so they are probably not reading quite the poem that Yeats wrote. And I would hope that all readers will resist adding the capital to "death", as was first done in the 1940 Macmillan text.

We now come to Yeats's letter to Higgins. Late in 1938 Yeats was planning a third series of Cuala Press *Broadsides*. Writing to Higgins on 22 November [1938], he told him "When I left Penns in

---

[31] Had the *London Mercury* been publishing prose or perhaps the work of a less famous poet, regularisation according to house style would of course be a fourth possibility. But the *London Mercury* would hardly have modified Yeats's poems in 1938.

[32] The version in LDW 181–3, an early text, omits the comma at l. 5 but includes one at l. 19; ll. 29–30 are different from the final text.

the Rocks eight days ago Dorothy [Wellesley] had selected half a dozen poems & her friend Hilda Matheson was doing the correspondence with authors etc". He also told Higgins that "on attached sheet are some amendations [sic] for that poem of mine to make it more suitable for singing":

Stanza 1   line 2   insert "From" before "gunshot"
Stanza 1   line 4   insert "or" before "Leaves"
Stanza 2   First two lines should be

> "Though stiffer at a bargain
> Than any old jew man"

line 8   insert "or" before "banish"

Stanza 3   should read

> I have heard it said in chapel
>   That but for Adams sin
> Edens garden should still be there
>   And I be there within.
> No expectations fail there
>   No pleasing habits end,
> No man grows old, no girl grows cold
>   But friend still walks by friend;
> No quarrels over h'apense there
>   They pluck the trees for bread
> What shall I do etc

(Yeats's changes in the stanza have not been transcribed.)

The first problem is what text of the poem Yeats's emendations are keyed to. I have assumed that Higgins would have had a copy of the same version submitted to the *London Mercury*, and I have further assumed, as argued above, that the *London Mercury* is an accurate text. Thus, for Yeats's emendations to the first two stanzas the only difficulty is the capitalisation of "Jew". With the third stanza, however, we must face an additional problem: should the punctuation of Yeats's letter to Higgins totally replace the punctuation of the *London Mercury*, or should the new passage be adopted to the punctuation of the periodical text? Although there are good arguments for either solution, I have adopted the second and have thus added punctuation at the end of ll. 31 and 34.

In sum, then, the text in the new *Poems* admits the following emendations to the "pure" text which would be produced by using the *London Mercury* as emended in Yeats's letter for parts I—II and Yeats's letter only for part III:

14: "Jew" has been capitalised, as in the *London Mercury*.

26: "Adams" has been corrected to "Adam's", as in the *London Mercury*.

27: "Edens" has been corrected to "Eden's", as in the *London Mercury*.

31: a comma has been added after "cold," as in the *London Mercury*.

33: "h'apense" has been corrected to "ha'pence".

34: a period has been added after "bread." All published editions as well as the final corrected typescript read "Who quarrels over halfpennies / That plucks the trees for bread?" There is little doubt that Yeats wanted a full stop before the refrain.[33]

"High Talk"

The text in the new *Poems* is taken from the *London Mercury* for December 1938. I have admitted one emendation:

4: "fench" has been corrected to "fence", the reading of the final corrected carbon typescript in the National Library of Ireland, marked "correct Sept 25", and *The Nation* (10 December 1938).

The 4—4—2—4 spacing arrangement for this sonnet in couplets is supported by the last two typescripts in the National Library of Ireland.[34] In one of her copies of *Last Poems & Plays*, Mrs Yeats

---

[33] There is an uncorrected carbon typescript of the poem in the collection of Michael B. Yeats, contained in an envelope marked by Mrs Yeats "Broadsides 1939—40". This follows the Cuala edition with one minor exception and was obviously prepared by Mrs Yeats after Yeats's death for the new series of Broadsides. Either Higgins failed to inform her of the revisions which Yeats had sent to him on 22 November [1938], or they chose to ignore them.

[34] In the *London Mercury* the space between ll. 10 and 11 coincides with the end of p. 114 and the beginning of p. 115. VP 623 fails to recognise this as a stanza division and thus has the break occurring only in *The Nation*.

changed "Daddy-long-legs" (l. 6) to "Daddy-longlegs", but the revision was fortunately not made in the 1949 *Poems*. I have no idea why "stories" (l. 7) was changed to "storeys" in the Macmillan *Last Poems & Plays*.

"The Apparitions"

The text in the new *Poems* follows that of the *London Mercury* for December 1938. No emendations have been required.

The lack of a comma after "length" (l. 19) is supported by the final corrected typescript in the National Library of Ireland, marked "correct August 12", by both periodical editions, and by the Cuala proofs.

"A Nativity"

The text in the new *Poems* is taken from the *London Mercury* for December 1938. No emendations have been required.

The only interesting variant in the final corrected typescript in the National Library of Ireland, marked "correct August 12", is the reading of l. 4: "Not a man, but Delacroix".

"Man and the Echo"

The text in the new *Poems* follows that of the *London Mercury* for January 1939. No emendations have been admitted.

The textual problems in this poem centre around the discrepancies between the *London Mercury* version and that in the *Atlantic Monthly* (January 1939). The American text offers "was wrecked" rather than "lay wrecked" (l. 16), "drugs" rather than "drug" (l. 26), "thoughts" rather than "thought" (l. 46), and numerous differences in punctuation (ll. 25, 37, 40–3, 45). The final corrected carbon typescript in the National Library of Ireland is identical to the *Atlantic Monthly* in "was wrecked" and "thoughts", but not in "drugs" or the added comma in l. 25. However, this final typescript (the last of four) is of little help in terms of the differences in punctuation in the final stanza, as at that point it is essentially free of punctuation, as is the third typescript.

Apparently Yeats considered the final stanza finished on the second typescript, to which he had added punctuation as follows:

> O rocky voice
> Shall we in that great night rejoice
> What do we know but that we face
> One another in this place?
> But hush, for I have lost the theme
> Its joy or night seem but a dream.
> Up there some hawk or owl has struck,
> Dropping out of sky or rock;
> A stricken rabbit is crying out
> And its cry distracts my thought.

It seems evident, then, that the typescript which Yeats prepared for publication in the autumn of 1938 must have had further refinements in the punctuation of the stanza. Again, based on the fact that Yeats had no direct role in the poem's appearance in the *Atlantic Monthly* and on the probability that he read proofs for the *London Mercury*, I have preferred the English text.[35]

Incidentally, on all four typescripts the title of the poem is "Man and the Echo". I know of no evidence favouring "The Man and the Echo", which first appears on the Cuala proofs.

"The Circus Animals' Desertion"

The text in the new *Poems* is taken from the *London Mercury* for January 1939. The following emendations have been admitted:

---

[35] In *Vision and Revision*, p. 72, Stallworthy describes the *Atlantic Monthly* text as the "first printing" and argues that "having seen it in print he [Yeats] made two further alterations . . . for its second printing in *The London Mercury* (also January 1939)". Given the role of Scott-James in placing the poem in America, the state of transatlantic mail service in 1938, and the fact that the *London Mercury* text was in print by 30 December 1938, this seems quite impossible. Stallworthy is also incorrect when he writes that "no advances are made" (p. 72) on the final typescript in the National Library of Ireland (folios N–O): Yeats added the "his" in l. 30.

There is an early version of "Man and the Echo" in LDW 179–81. Stallworthy suggests (p. 70) that Yeats copied this out for Wellesley, but I suspect that her notation of "copied at Penns" means just the opposite, that she copied the poem itself − which would explain why her version lacks ll. 41–2.

Title: "Animal's" has been corrected to "Animals'", as on all four typescripts in the National Library of Ireland.

10: "Usheen" has been regularised to "Oisin", Yeats's preferred form in the 1933 *Collected Poems*.

26: "Cuchullain" has been regularised to "Cuchulain", Yeats's preferred form since 1904.

The *London Mercury* version is very close to the corrected final carbon typescript in the National Library of Ireland, marked "correct Sept 23". The major difference is that on the typescript Yeats cancelled the title "The Circus Animals' Desertion", replaced it by "Despair", and then replaced that by "On the lack of a theme".

In *Yeats at Work*, Curtis Bradford has argued that the proper reading in l. 26 is "invulnerable", as on the last holograph manuscript, rather than "ungovernable", which appears in all the typescripts, the Cuala proofs, and all published texts. Bradford is certain that "his typist made the mistake, and Yeats may never have noticed it, given the eye's uncanny ability to see what it expects rather than what is on the page".[36] This is indeed possible, especially in the light of the use of "invulnerable" in "Cuchulain's Fight with the Sea" (l. 86), *Fighting the Waves* (l. 554), and *The Death of Cuchulain* (l. 1059). However, as Bradford admits, the holograph manuscript is quite clear, and it would not have been easy for anyone to have misread "invulnerable". Indeed, I suspect that the first typescript may well have been prepared from dictation and that Yeats made the revision during the process. In any event, it is certain that on three different typescripts and a carbon of one of them, the reading is "ungovernable"; and on each of the four typescripts Yeats has made some change in either ll. 25, 26, or 27. I have thus decided against the emendation.

"Politics"

The text in the new *Poems* is taken from the *London Mercury* for January 1939. No emendations have been required.

Since there are significant differences between the final heavily corrected typescript in the National Library of Ireland, marked "correct August 12", and the *London Mercury* version − including

---

[36] *Yeats at Work*, p. 162.

"this girl" rather than "that girl" (l. 1) and "has read and thought" rather than "has both read and thought" (l. 8) — Yeats must have further refined the poem before submitting copy or have made corrections on proof.

It is perhaps all too symbolic that in what was intended to stand as the final poem in the volume which Yeats was preparing at the time of his death, one of the emendations made by Mrs Yeats or Thomas Mark for *Last Poems & Plays*, "meanings" to "meaning" in the epigraph, should result in a mis-quotation.[37]

[37] Yeats's source for the epigraph was Archibald MacLeish's "Public Speech and Private Speech in Poetry", *Yale Review*, 27, No. 3 (March 1938), 545–6: "Thomas Mann, who has reason to know, says of the nature of our time, that in our time the destiny of man presents its meanings in political terms." Cf. L 908–9.

There are two early versions of "Politics" in LDW 163–5.

CHAPTER SIX

Other Poems

A. Early Poems

For those early lyrics which Yeats never included in one of his collections, the text in the new *Poems* follows the first publication. Some of these poems were reprinted in various Christmas numbers of *The Irish Homestead*, which was edited by Yeats's friend George W. Russell (AE), but it is altogether unlikely that Yeats was responsible for the variants in those editions. Writing to Lady Gregory on 12 December 1902 about the appearance in the journal of "She Who Dwelt among the Sycamores", for example, Yeats complained that

> No! I don't like that Sycamore poem, I think it perfectly detestable and always did and am going to write to Russell to say that the *Homestead* musn't do this kind of thing any more. I was furious last year when they revived some rambling old verses of mine but forgot about it. I wouldn't so much mind if they said they were early verses but they print them as if they were new work. (L 390)[1]

Likewise, there is little chance that Yeats was involved in the reprinting of "Mourn—And Then Onward!" in *The Irish Weekly Independent* for 20 May 1893. In the case of the one poem that Yeats did contribute to *The Irish Weekly Independent*, "The Ballad of Earl Paul" in the inaugural issue (8 April 1893), it is clear that the newspaper text includes two misprints. These have been corrected in the new *Poems* as follows:

l. 67: "dweft" has been emended to "dwelt".

[1] Yeats refers to the printing of "The Fairy Thorn" in the Christmas number of the 1901 *Irish Homestead*. The poem had first been published in *The Irish Monthly* for March 1887.

l. 68: the comma at the end of the poem has been changed to a period.

However, most of the textual problems in the early poems concern those works which were last published in *The Wanderings of Oisin and Other Poems* (1889). In that collection Yeats included a slightly revised version of Act II, Scene III, of *The Island of Statues*, the entire play having first been published serially in the *Dublin University Review* from April–July 1885. It seems evident that there are several misprints in the 1889 version. In the new *Poems* these have been corrected in accord with the periodical text:

l. 55: "before her shepherd hair / Had left the island breeze" has been emended to the earlier "felt the island breeze".

l. 213: "In those fair years" has been emended to the earlier "far years".

l. 295: In the *Dublin University Review* the passage reads "A rover I, who come from where men's ears / Love storm; and stained with mist the new moons flare." Yeats revised this to eliminate the punctuation, but in the process "moons" was somehow changed to "moon's", a reading which does not make sense.

The other textual problems in these early poems are connected with the existence of several corrected copies of *The Wanderings of Oisin and Other Poems*. Writing to Thomas Mark on 8 April 1949, Mrs Yeats explained that

When I was in London in 1942 I found in a bookshop in Charing Cross Shop Road a copy of WANDERINGS OF OISIN inscribed "W B Yeats This copy is not to be lent as I have made corrections in it that I do not want to lose." I should like you to have it as a token of gratitude for your many years of sensitive care in seeing WBY's work through the press.

Mark acknowledged receipt of this gift in a letter of 22 April 1949, indicating that he would be "very pleased and proud to possess" the volume. This annotated copy remained in Mark's possession until his death in 1963, after which it was sold by his widow to a private collector, reportedly an American. As with Yeats's September 1932

letter to Mark about his poems, its present whereabouts is unknown.[2]

This copy of the collection is the source of the privately printed
edition of *Mosada* issued by the Cuala Press in 1943. The colophon
explains that the play was printed "from the text of 1889 published
in THE WANDERINGS OF OSIN with the manuscript corrections made by the author on his own copy".[3] The collection of
Michael B. Yeats includes a typescript of the version of *Mosada*
published in the *Dublin University Review* (June 1886), on which
Mrs Yeats has made notes of the variants in the annotated copy.
Since she was making corrections to the wrong edition, there are
some problems in incorporating all of her changes in the new
Poems, as we shall see.[4] Moreover, those corrections must be
balanced against Yeats's markings in two other annotated copies
of *The Wanderings of Oisin* which have come to light. Reading
University has a copy of the volume from the collection of Edwin J.
Ellis, Yeats's collaborator on the 1893 edition of Blake. This is
signed by Yeats with the notation "corrections in this book made at
my dictation" and dated "May 7. 1889".[5] The Robert H. Taylor
Collection at the Princeton University Library has a copy signed
"Edward Garnett from W B Yeats Sept 26 1890". Some of the revisions in the two books overlap with each other, or with the nota-
tions on the *Mosada* typescript; others are found only in one copy;
and in two instances a choice must be made between different
corrections to the same line. The annotations in question are as
follows:

A. *Mosada*, epigraph
   The typescript indicates that Yeats deleted the epigraph,
"And my Lord Cardinal hath had strange days in his youth",
ascribed to "a Memoir of the Fifteenth Century". The source of

---

[2] I am grateful to Warwick Gould for information about his interview with Mrs
   Thomas Mark and to Richard Garnett for his attempts to acquire further knowledge about the sale of the material. Jon Stallworthy saw the annotated copy
   when he was working on *Between the Lines* but did not take notes on it.
[3] *Mosada* (privately printed, Dublin: Cuala Press, 1943), p. [21].
[4] Despite the statement in the colophon, this typescript must have been used as
   copy by the Cuala Press, and thus there are a number of incorrect readings in
   their edition. For example, at III.101 the early "is thy head" appears in the
   1943 volume, rather than "lies thy head", a change which Yeats made for *The
   Wanderings of Oisin and Other Poems*.
[5] I am grateful to Ian Fletcher for informing me of this copy and for providing
   copies of the annotated pages.

the epigraph has yet to be traced, and it is not impossible that it was in fact invented by Yeats. One might note that for *The Wanderings of Oisin and Other Poems* Yeats changed Ebremar's former name from "Vallence" to "Gomez".

B. *Mosada*, I, 38
   The typescript revises "comes" to "rises".

C. *Mosada*, I, 97
   The typescript changes "ha! ha! they come, they come!" to "they come, they come, they come!"

D. *Mosada*, II, 23
   The typescript revises "Beside" to "By".

E. *Mosada*, II, 24
   The typescript changes "Then he shouted" to "The stranger shouted".

F. *Mosada*, II, 42
   The Princeton copy revises "wages" to "wage", a change also made on the typescript.

G. *Mosada*, II, 42
   In the early text used for the typescript, the line ends with a single "No use", rather than the 1889 version, "No use. No good". Mrs Yeats has added "No use" in the margin of the typescript, apparently indicating that it should replace "No good", as was done for the 1943 *Mosada*. This reading has been adopted in the new *Poems*.

H. *Mosada*, III, 5
   The early text used for the typescript reads "Soft as a long dead footstep whispering through", rather than the version in *The Wanderings of Oisin and Other Poems*, "Soft as the whispering of a long-lost footstep". Mrs Yeats has indicated that "long" should be deleted. That such a deletion applies to the 1889 text is confirmed by the cancellation of "long" in the Reading copy.

I. *Mosada*, III, 6
   The early text used for the typescript reads "The brain. My brothers will be passing down", rather than the 1889 version, "Circling the brain? My brothers will pass down". Mrs Yeats has indicated that "will" should be changed to "now", and the 1943

edition therefore reads "now pass down". On the Reading copy, though, Yeats has added "now" after "will", thus "will now pass down". Since we do not know the date of the corrections which Mrs Yeats is working from, a certain choice is impossible. In the new *Poems* I have adopted her reading, "now pass down". However, there seems to be no support for the lack of a capital on "My" in the Cuala Press volume.

J. *Mosada*, III, 7

Both the typescript and the Reading copy change "Quite soon the cornfield" to "Along the cornfield".

K. *Mosada*, III, 10

The typescript, the Reading copy, and the Princeton copy all revise "Will be" to "Will move", the unique instance of identical revision.

L. *Mosada*, III, 12

The typescript deletes "scarcely" before "dawning".

M. *Mosada*, III, 13

In *The Wanderings of Oisin and Other Poems*, the first part of the line reads "And Hassan will be with them". Mrs Yeats (whose typescript has the error "Cola" for "Hassan") has indicated that the line should read "Hassan is with them too"; the same revision is found in the Reading copy. However, in the Princeton copy Yeats has revised the line to "And Hassan will be one". Again, a definite choice is difficult without knowing the date of the copy Mrs Yeats was using. In the new *Poems* I have adopted the majority reading of "Hassan is with them too".

N. *Mosada*, III, [40A]–41

Both the typescript and the Princeton copy change "Yonder a leaf / Of apple-blossom" to simply "An apple-blossom", thereby eliminating what had been l. 41. There is no support for the lack of a hyphen in "apple-blossom" in the Cuala Press edition.

O. *Mosada*, III, 58

The Reading copy revises "I cannot even crawl along the flags" to "I cannot even crawl along the stones". Apparently the same change was made in the annotated copy of *The Wanderings of Oisin and Other Early Poems* that Mrs Yeats was using, but she was unsure of the reading and therefore marked "stones?"

on the typescript. The revision was not made for the 1943 printing.

P. *Mosada*, III, 78
The Reading copy changes "Afar along" to "Far, far along".

Q. "How Ferencz Renyi Kept Silent", l. 106
The Reading copy revises "Assassin, my assassin!" to "Assassin, assassin!"

R. "She Who Dwelt among the Sycamores", l. 9
The Reading copy changes "the six feet" to "all their feet".

S. "She Who Dwelt among the Sycamores", l. 11
The Reading copy revises "four eyes droop low" to "their eyes droop low".

T. "Quatrains and Aphorisms", ll. 21, 24
Both the Reading and Princeton copies eliminate the quotation marks around the stanza.

It should be added that both the Princeton and Reading copies of *The Wanderings of Oisin and Other Poems* contain numerous other revisions which have not been adopted in the new *Poems* since they were made to works which Yeats himself later republished.[6] Whether the copy which Mrs Yeats used to correct the typescript of *Mosada* had corrections to other poems, it is now impossible to say. On the one hand, it is likely that she would have compiled a list of such corrections before giving the book to Thomas Mark, and no such list is known to survive. On the other hand, in his letter to her acknowledging the gift, Mark wrote "I see now that the text of OISIN is quite different from the later versions, so that it does not affect Vol. I of the limited POEMS", a statement which might be taken to mean that the copy did include corrections to at least "The Wanderings of Oisin".

B. Poems from the Plays

For all but four late plays, the basic text followed in the new *Poems* is the Macmillan, London, edition of the *Collected Plays*, published

---

[6] In one instance Yeats published a revised text of a poem from *The Wanderings of Oisin* in a periodical but thereafter excluded it from his collections: "Street Dancers" appeared in a revised form in *The Leisure Hour* (April 1890), 319–20, the source of the text in the new *Poems*.

on 30 November 1934. Yeats carefully read the final page proofs for that collection (now in British Library Additional Manuscripts 55879, with date-stamps from 5 July–9 August 1934), and he made numerous small revisions. For example, in "What message comes to famous Thebes from the Golden House?", from _Sophocles' King Oedipus_, Yeats added the capital on "God" (ll. 6, 11, 15), the hyphen in "anchor-fluke" (l. 15), and the comma after "head" (l. 17), and he also caught the misprint of "towsel" for "tousle" (l. 21). For our purposes there are no discrepancies between these corrected proofs and the published _Collected Plays_.

The lyrics from _The King of the Great Clock Tower_ and _A Full Moon in March_ are taken from the Macmillan, London, edition of _A Full Moon in March_ (1935). Although both plays were reprinted in the Macmillan, New York, edition of _The Herne's Egg and Other Plays_ (1938), it is unlikely that Yeats had much to do with the production of that volume aside from contributing a Preface. In any event, as far as the lyrics from the plays are concerned, the only important variant is l. 5 of "I sing a song of Jack and Jill" from _A Full Moon in March_, where _The Herne's Egg and Other Plays_ uses a comma at the end of the line instead of the period found in _A Full Moon in March_.[7] Yeats had significantly revised the lyric from its printing in _Poetry_ for the 1935 edition, and it is improbable that he returned to it again for the 1938 text.

The poems from _The Herne's Egg_ are taken from Yeats's corrected copy of _The Herne's Egg: A Stage Play_, issued by Macmillan, London, on 21 January 1938. Sending the text of the play to Thomas Mark on 7 June 1939, Mrs Yeats explained that Yeats "had made a certain number of additions in his own copy, and I have copied these into the copy I send". Yeats's corrections did

---

[7] In _The Herne's Egg and Other Plays_ (New York: Macmillan, 1938), p. 129, there is no stanza break between ll. 6–7 of ["O, what may come"] in _The King of the Great Clock Tower_. However, the break is found in all three printings of the first version of the play: _Life and Letters_, 11, No. 59 (November 1934), 144; _The King of the Great Clock Tower_ (Dublin: Cuala, 1934), p. 7; and _The King of the Great Clock Tower_ (New York: Macmillan, 1935), p. 9. In the revised text first published in _A Full Moon in March_ (London: Macmillan, 1935), the break coincides with pp. 36–7. It is therefore unlikely that the lack of a break in the 1938 edition is an authorised change.

The Variorum Edition of the Plays of W. B. Yeats, ed. Russell K. Alspach (New York: Macmillan, 1966), p. 1000, errs in not recognising the stanza division in the three printings of the first version of the play. The corrected second printing (1966) of _Variorum Plays_ hereafter cited VP1.

not include the two variants between the contemporary editions of
the play and the version published in the Macmillan, London,
1952 *Collected Plays*: the addition of a comma at the end of l. 1 of
"This they nailed upon a post" and the change from a comma to a
question mark at the end of l. 14 of "When I take a beast to my joy-
ful breast". These emendations have therefore not been admitted
into the new *Poems*.

The text of the closing lyric from *The Death of Cuchulain* is
taken from the final contemporary typescript in National Library
of Ireland MS. 8772. As Phillip L. Marcus has established in his
edition of the manuscripts of the play, "typescript No. 7, on which
Mrs Yeats wrote out (possibly from Yeats's dictation) the revised
version of TS6, is marked 'corrected Jan · 22 1939'; thus it predates
her husband's death and its divergences from TS6 could have
received authorial sanction".[8] The following emendations have
been admitted:

l. 3: "Conal" has been emended to "Conall", Yeats's spelling
in the revised version of *The Green Helmet* as well as in one of
his major sources, Lady Gregory's *Cuchulain of Muirthemne*.

ll. 3, 23: "Cuchullain" has been regularised to "Cuchulain",
Yeats's preferred form since 1904.

l. 6: the typing error "Adore" has been corrected to "adore".

l. 8: the period after "thighs" has been added.

l. 12: the period after "men" has been added.

l. 16: the period after "loathe" has been added.

Many readers will doubtless prefer the further emendations found
in the Cuala Press *Last Poems and Two Plays*, but the manuscripts
provide no support for the additional punctuation. Nor, as
Marcus notes, is there any evidence favouring the omission in the
Variorum Plays of "back" in "But an old man looking back on life"
(l. 27).[9]

If, however, the textual problems in the poems from the plays are
less than extensive, there are other concerns which merit discussion.

[8] The Death of Cuchulain: *Manuscript Materials, including the Author's Final Text*, ed. Phillip L. Marcus (Ithaca and London: Cornell University Press, 1982), p. 167. I am indebted to Marcus for a copy of the typescript of his edition in advance of publication.

[9] Marcus, p. 182.

First is the question of whether *all* the songs and lyrics should be
included in any new edition of Yeats's poems. It was Yeats's
practice throughout his career to publish separately some of the
poems from his plays, either in a journal and/or a collection of his
verse. A few of these survived through the *Collected Poems* or *A
Full Moon in March*: to cite the examples from both ends of his
career, the "Crossways" section of the 1895 *Poems* included "The
Cloak, the Boat, and the Shoes", originally a lyric in *The Island of
Statues*; and *A Full Moon in March* contained not only the
"Alternative Song for the Severed Head in 'The King of the Great
Clock Tower'" but also a revised version of a song from *The Pot of
Broth* and an expanded version of a song from *The Player Queen*,
printed under the title "Two Songs Rewritten for the Tune's
Sake". An example of a lyric which did not survive through the
Collected Poems is the poem from *At the Hawk's Well* published as
"The Well and the Tree" in the 1916 *Responsibilities and Other
Poems* but not thereafter published separately. Considering that
Yeats does not seem to have formulated a consistent policy on the
matter, I have decided in favour of inclusiveness and have in-
cluded all of the songs and lyrics from the plays.[10]

A second problem concerns the authorship of these poems.
Many of Yeats's plays were written in collaboration with Lady
Gregory, the exact share of her contribution being a matter of
some controversy in Yeats studies. But just as Yeats contributed a
song to her *The Travelling Man*, she may well have written — or at
least drafted — a considerable number of the poems in "Yeats's"
plays. Given the nature of their collaboration, as well as the state
of the surviving manuscripts (a manuscript in Lady Gregory's
hand, for instance, could have been dictated by Yeats), it seems
essentially impossible to assign a particular passage to one or the
other. It should also be added that several other writers are known

---

[10] In printing the poems from the plays in the new *Poems*, I have eliminated all
stage directions; in most cases, those occurring between lines have been treated
as constituting stanza divisions. Inevitably, some arbitrary decisions on those
and other matters have had to be made, but I have attempted to follow Yeats's
own practice when he printed the songs from his plays as separate poems. To
cite just one instance, it seems clear that ["Do not make a great keening"] and
["They shall be remembered for ever"] should be considered two songs rather
than one, as the music provided for them is different (see *Plays in Prose and
Verse* [London: Macmillan, 1922], p. 447). David R. Clark's forthcoming
edition of *Plays* will of course provide accurate texts for the poems in the plays
in their original setting.

or suspected collaborators with Yeats, with Douglas Hyde having
one of the strongest claims.[11]

A third and related problem is the question of those poems
which are derived from Gaelic sources. Here not only must we
wonder whether Yeats had any hand in the translation itself but
also we must deal with the thorny question of when a "translation"
becomes sufficiently distinct from the original as to be considered
a "new" poem.[12] My policy in the new *Poems* has been that any
substantive change from the original is sufficient to admit the work
into the edition. Such would seem to be Yeats's own attitude
towards his work of this kind. The most famous example is, of
course, "Down by the Salley Gardens", which in its first publication read as follows:

Down by the salley gardens my love and I did meet;
She passed the salley gardens with little snow-white feet.
She bid me take love easy as the leaves grow easy on the tree;
But I, being young and foolish, with her would not agree.

In a field by the river my love and I did stand,
And on my leaning shoulder she laid her snow-white hand.
She bid me take life easy as the grass grows on the weirs;
But I was young and foolish, and now am full of tears.

(VP 90)

Yeats claimed that the poem was "an attempt to reconstruct an old

---

[11] See, for example, Vivian Mercier, "Douglas Hyde's 'Share' in *The Unicorn from the Stars*", *Modern Drama*, 7, No. 4 (February 1965), 463–5.

One of the queries which Mark sent Mrs Yeats in 1939 concerned the quotation marks around the songs in *The Unicorn from the Stars*: "My own opinion
is that the songs in *The Unicorn* need not have 'quote' to distinguish them from
Mr. Yeats's own lyrics. On the same principle we ought to have them for the
quotations from Shelley, etc, in the prose works. I think that it would look
rather queer, but I would rather follow your judgment in this matter. If the
quotes were only required in this one play, where their purpose would be plain,
they might as well go in." Mrs Yeats replied as follows when she returned the
list of queries to Mark on 5 July 1939: "*Only* in this play – It was the only play
containing songs not written by WBY." As we shall see, that statement is not
altogether accurate.

[12] In "The Sources of James Stephens's *Reincarnations*: 'Alone I did it, barring
for the noble assistance of the gods'", *Tulane Studies in English*, 22 (1977),
143–53, I attempted to deal with this question in the work of another Anglo-
Irish writer by using Dryden's terms of "metaphrase", "paraphrase", and
"imitation".

song from three lines imperfectly remembered by an old peasant
woman in the village of Ballysodare, Sligo, who often sings them to
herself' (VP 90). However, as Michael B. Yeats has remarked, "it
is quite clear that the old peasant woman of Ballysodare must have
remembered far more than three lines of this old folk song", his
evidence being a manuscript in the P. J. McCall Ballad Collection
in the National Library of Ireland.[13]

Down by the Sally Gardens my own true love and I did meet
She passed the Sally Gardens, a tripping with her snow white
    feet.
She bid me take life easy just as leaves fall from each tree;
But I being young and foolish with my true love would not
    agree.

In a field by the river my lovely girl and I did stand.
And leaning on her shoulder I pressed her burning hand.
She bid me take life easy, just as the stream flows o'er the
    weirs
But I being young and foolish I parted her that day in tears.

I wish I was in Banagher and my fine girl upon my knee.
And I with money plenty to keep her in good company.
I'd call for liquor of the best with flowing bowls on every
    side.
Kind fortune ne'er shall daunt me, I am young and the
    world's wide.

As for the omission by Yeats of the third stanza, one can only agree
with Michael B. Yeats: "it may be that the woman of Ballysodare

---

[13] Michael B. Yeats, "W. B. Yeats and Irish Folk Song", *Southern Folklore
Quarterly*, 30, No. 2 (June 1966), 158. The entire article (pp. 153–78) is
relevant to the present discussion. Here and in Appendix B I am indebted to it
and to the following: Roger McHugh, "James Joyce's Synge-Song", *Envoy*, 3,
No. 12 (November 1950), 12–17; Michael B. Yeats, "Words and Music", *The
Yeats Society of Japan: Annual Report*, No. 8 (1973), 7–18; Colin Meir, *The
Ballads and Songs of W. B. Yeats: The Anglo-Irish Heritage in Subject and
Style* (London: Macmillan, 1974), passim; Ole Munch-Pedersen, "Yeats's
Synge-Song", *Irish University Review*, 6, No. 2 (Autumn 1976), 204–13; and
James Stewart, "Three That Are Watching My Time To Run", *Irish Uni-
versity Review*, 9, No. 1 (Spring 1979), 112–18. Munch-Pedersen and Stewart
are particularly helpful in providing full information on the translations
available to Yeats.

really had forgotten this verse, but it is perhaps more likely that he thought it inferior to the rest of the song, and so left it out."[14]

"Down by the Salley Gardens" is only one example of a poem produced by Yeats's reworking of an original source. Others include "Love Song. / From the Gaelic", published only in *Poems and Ballads of Young Ireland* (1888) and based on a translation in Edward Walsh's introduction to *Irish Popular Songs* (see L 47, n. 3); "When You Are Old", from Ronsard's "Quand vous serez bien vieille" (*Sonnets pour Hélène*, II, 43); "A Drinking Song", from Lady Gregory's adaptation of Goldoni's *La Locandiera*; and "Swift's Epitaph", from the Latin inscription on Swift's tomb in St Patrick's Cathedral, Dublin. For our purposes, what is important is not the degree of fidelity to the original for any particular poem, but the fact that Yeats was willing to present such works as his own (four of the five examples above were included by Yeats in his standard canon).

In Appendix B I have listed sources for those poems from the plays which have been included in the new *Poems* (there is of course no question about the inclusion of the first of "Two Songs Rewritten for the Tune's Sake", which Yeats himself placed in *A Full Moon in March*). This Appendix also provides information on the two slightly modified quotations and the single quatrain which have been excluded from the new edition because of the lack of any substantive alteration by Yeats. Given the kind of sources available to Yeats, especially the knowledge of folk songs by Lady Gregory and Hyde, it is by no means certain that the source listed is *the* source: my aim has simply been to provide an English source available to Yeats at the appropriate time. If future research uncovers a source which is identical to the text used by Yeats, then the poem in question should, I suggest, be eliminated from the canon.

---

[14] "W. B. Yeats and Irish Folk Song", p. 159. Michael B. Yeats also notes that it was Arthur Perceval Graves's 1894 *Irish Song Book* which "first set Yeats's 'Down by the Salley Gardens' to music. He simplified the folk tune, with a view perhaps to making it easier to sing. In Graves's setting the song has gained great popularity, and has quite displaced the folk original. The folk version was at one time known all over Ireland, and had no especial connection with Sligo, but the popularity of Yeats's song has nowadays quite changed this position. The good people of Sligo have now in fact discovered a grove of willow trees which are, they say, the original Salley Gardens of the song, and these are shown with pride to foreign visitors to the district. Thus are traditions made" (p. 159).

C. Poems from the Prose Fiction

The text of "Full moody is my love and sad" from the short story "Dhoya" has been taken from the 1908 *Collected Works in Verse & Prose*, the last printing in Yeats's lifetime. For "Out of sight is out of mind" (from "The Wisdom of the King"), "The poet, Owen Hanrahan, under a bush of may" (from "Red Hanrahan's Curse") and "Seven paters seven times" (from "The Adoration of the Magi"), the text used is the final corrected page proofs for the volume of *Mythologies* in the Edition de Luxe. Yeats returned these proofs to the publishers on 5 July 1932, noting that he "need not see" them again (55003/129). These proofs have been adopted as the basic text for the new variorum edition of *The Secret Rose*.[15]

Thus the only interesting textual problem concerning the poems from the prose fiction is again a matter of "translation". The source of the poem in "The Adoration of the Magi" is Domhnall Ó Fotharta's *Siasma an Gheimhridh* (1892).[16] Yeats may have learned of this work from Douglas Hyde, who later included a version of the poem in his *Religious Songs of Connacht*.[17] Yeats uses only the first eight lines of the twelve-line poem. Included in "The Adoration of the Magi" is an inaccurate version of the Gaelic text itself. As Brendan P. O Hehir has explained to me, Yeats's "transcript was made by someone very insecure with Irish (himself?)".[18] The translation offered in the story is as follows:

> Seven paters seven times,
> Send Mary by her Son,
> Send Bridget by her mantle,
> Send God by His strength,
> Between us and the fairy host,
> Between us and the demons of the air.

---

[15] *The Secret Rose, Stories by W. B. Yeats: A Variorum Edition*, ed. Phillip L. Marcus, Warwick Gould, and Michael J. Sidnell (Ithaca and London: Cornell University Press, 1981). See esp. pp. xvii–xxix.

[16] I am grateful to Warwick Gould for sharing with me his correspondence about the poem with Francis John Byrne and Kevin Danaher, the latter of whom first traced the source.

[17] Douglas Hyde, *Religious Songs of Connacht* (London: T. Fisher Unwin; Dublin: M. H. Gill and Son, 1906), II, 50–3. Hyde's translation was first published in the *New Ireland Review*, 12, No. 4 (December 1899), 256.

[18] Letter from Brendan P. O Hehir to Richard J. Finneran, 19 October 1980. I must once again thank Professor O Hehir, who has been providing me with information about Yeats's use of Gaelic since my 1969 edition of *John Sherman and Dhoya*, for his speedy and detailed response to my queries.

O Hehir describes this version as "possible . . . only for somebody with the most sketchy knowledge of the language", which would be a good description of Yeats's condition at the time. Certainly it is too inaccurate to be the work of Hyde. O Hehir's literal translation is as follows:

> Seven prayers times seven
> Mary entrusted to her son,
> Brigid entrusted to her cloak,
> God entrusted to his strength,
> Between us and the Host of the Mounds,
> Between us and the Host of the Wind.

It is doubtless ironic that what is presented as a direct translation in "The Adoration of the Magi" shows more variation from the original than some of the songs from the plays discussed above. Nevertheless, it is not impossible to suppose that Yeats intended the alterations, and the fact remains that the poem as it stands in the story is by no means a straightforward translation. "Seven paters seven times" has therefore been included – not without reluctance – in the new *Poems*.

D. Poems from *On the Boiler*

The source of the texts in the new *Poems* is British Library Additional Manuscripts 55881, which includes the second set of corrected page proofs. As we shall see, there are only minor differences between these proofs and the first edition of *On the Boiler*.[19]

Before Yeats left Dublin on 8 or 9 July 1938, he had given the typescript of *On the Boiler* to F. R. Higgins, "who is to send it to the printer" (L 912; see LDW 169 for the date of Yeats's departure from Ireland). On 4 September 1938 he was able to inform Edith Shackleton Heald that "*On the Boiler* has at last gone to press" (L 915). At some point in the fall of 1938, Yeats must have read galley proofs. The chronology thereafter becomes cloudy, but I

---

[19] VP 625–8 does not take into account the variants between the first and second editions of *On the Boiler*. Alspach may have been following Wade's statement in the *Bibliography* (p. 202) that "the contents" of the second printing "are the same as those of" the first.

believe that he must have received the first set of page proofs shortly after he arrived in France in late November 1938. In an undated letter to Higgins from Cap Martin, Yeats wrote as follows:

> Paged proofs came some days ago and my wife and I have spent a good deal of our time at them. I think we have now corrected everything, but I think it probable that when you look through them you will decide that another revise is necessary. There will be no need for it to be sent here if you would be so kind as to look through it. Indeed much of it is revisions of the press which should be done by somebody who can hear in a day or so by telephone. They have evidently never done printing of our kind before and get into great confusion. Indeed their errors are of a kind that I dont always know how to correct.
>
> They sent no proof of title page and I would be very much obliged if you would arrange about the cover. I enclose the cover paper I preferred. I enclose also their letter. My wife tells me that you have the estimeate [sic] they refer to.

Apparently Higgins did not respond to this letter with alacrity. Yeats told Heald on 22 December 1938 that "Higgins has dropped in a gulch. Owes me four letters — damn" (L 920). The next day he wrote Ethel Mannin that "This is the bother about *The Boiler*. Went to the printer seven months ago — small Longford printer selected in pure eccentricity by the poet Higgins — not yet out" (L 921). Finally, Yeats wrote to Higgins himself on 24 December 1938:

> You might let me know if you have received the proofs of 'On the Boiler'. I want *Purgatory* played from 'On the Boiler' version and the text in the hands of the public as soon as possible after the performance. I must of course correct my own proofs.

Higgins was now surely confused about Yeats's wishes concerning the further correction of the proofs. I conjecture that he returned the proofs to Yeats and suggested that it would be better if Yeats continue to deal directly with the printers. Yeats thus wrote to the Longford Printing Press on 10 January 1939:

> I return one set of page proofs corrected. Please send me a

revise to the above address, and return to me the *copy with my corrections*. I had a great deal of trouble in making these corrections because you did not return to me the corrected galley proofs when sending paged proof.

Have you yet received from Mr. F. R. Higgins the copy of the estimate you refer to in your last letter? I have asked him to send it to you.

I shall be glad to receive the revised page proof at your earliest convenience.

The Longford printers must have complied with Yeats's request. It is the revised set of proofs, with Yeats's further corrections, that was sent to Thomas Mark and which is now in the Macmillan Archive in the British Library.[20] Fragments of the first set of page proofs survive in the collections of Michael B. Yeats and the National Library of Ireland (MS. 8771). Other unique materials relevant to the three poems from *On the Boiler* include manuscripts and typescripts in the collections of Michael B. Yeats and the National Library of Ireland (MS. 13,569); and a manuscript of "[Crazy Jane on the Mountain]" and typescripts of "[Why should not Old Men be Mad?]" and "A Statesman's Holiday" in the Heald papers at Harvard University.

There are only minor textual problems in the three poems, as follows.

"[Why should not Old Men be Mad?]"

Yeats made no changes on the final page proofs, and the text is identical to that in the first edition of *On the Boiler*. The title is taken from the final typescript in the National Library of Ireland, marked by Yeats "correct August 12". There is no manuscript support for the reading in l. 9 of "Some think it a matter of chance", which first appears in *Last Poems & Plays*, rather than "Some think it matter of chance".

[20] This reconstruction differs substantially from that offered by Sandra F. Siegel in "Yeats's Quarrel with Himself: The Design and Argument of *On the Boiler*", pp. 352–3. However, as noted earlier (Chapter V, n. 2), Siegel was unaware of the proofs in the British Library, and it is unclear whether she recognised the differences between the two printings of *On the Boiler*. Siegel (p. 353, n. 15) places the undated letter from Yeats to Higgins after 24 December 1938. But the undated letter begins "I shall write to you about Cuala etc in a few days. For the moment I confine myself to the BOILER", and the letter of 24 December 1938 is primarily about forthcoming publications by the Cuala Press.

"[Crazy Jane on the Mountain]"

Yeats added the comma at the end of l. 9 on the final page proofs. This was overlooked by the Longford printers; otherwise the text is identical to the first edition of *On the Boiler*. The title is taken from the final corrected typescript in the National Library of Ireland, marked by Yeats "correct August 12". In the new *Poems* one emendation has been admitted:

> l. 17: "Cuchullain", the reading of both the final proofs and the first edition of *On the Boiler*, has been regularised to "Cuchulain", Yeats's preferred form since 1904.

"A Statesman's Holiday"

Yeats wrote in the title on the final page proofs. Earlier he had vacillated between "The Statesman's Holiday", as on the penultimate typescript in the National Library of Ireland, and "Avalon", as on the Heald typescript and the final corrected typescript in the National Library of Ireland, marked by Yeats "correct August 12".[21] Yeats added the accent mark on Valéra in l. 18, but this was overlooked by the Longford printers and does not appear in the first edition of *On the Boiler*. Also, next to l. 27, which on the proofs was the last line on p. 32, Yeats indicated "this line to go to top of next page". He wrote out the line at the top of p. 33 but failed to include the comma at the end of the line. However, the comma was used in the first edition of *On the Boiler*, and it has been included in the new *Poems*. It is doubtful whether this should be considered an emendation, but one certain change has been admitted into the new *Poems*:

> l. 6: "troup", the reading of all typescripts and proofs as well as the first edition of *On the Boiler*, has been emended to "troop", on the analogy of Yeats's change in "Roger Casement" of "Come Alfred Noyes and all the troup" (*The Irish Press*, 2 February 1937) to "Come Tom and Dick, come all the troop" (*New Poems*, 1938). The second edition of *On the Boiler* and *Last Poems & Plays* use "troop".

[21] Several other typescripts for works which were eventually published in *Last Poems and Two Plays* are also marked "correct August 12". Since at the time Yeats had already given the final typescript of *On the Boiler* to Higgins, the fact that he returned to the typescripts of the three poems from *On the Boiler* suggests that he might have planned to include them in his next collection of verse. However, as already noted (p. 65), they are not included on the draft table of contents for *Last Poems and Two Plays*.

E. Other Poems

Only a handful of poems have not yet been discussed. For most of them, there are no textual problems, and the Textual Notes in the new *Poems* indicate the source used, normally the last edition published in Yeats's lifetime. In the case of the six poems taken from *Wheels and Butterflies* (London: Macmillan, 1934), it has been possible to verify the printed texts against the material in British Library Additional Manuscripts 55878. The poems from the several Introductions are not marked on the proofs, and the printed versions are identical. On the proofs Thomas Mark suggested that the colon in "The bravest from the gods but ask: / A house, a sword, a ship, a mask" be eliminated; but Yeats did not respond, and the colon carries over into the published text. "To a Garret or Cellar a wheel I send, / But every butterfly to a friend" is not included on the extant proofs; the typescript lacks the comma, which must have been added on those missing proofs.

Thus there are only two poems with significant textual problems which remain to be examined. The first is "The Blood Bond" from *Diarmuid and Grania*, published separately in *A Broad Sheet* for January 1902. Given the title, the action in the play preceding the lyric, and the illustration in *A Broad Sheet* showing Finn holding up a cup made from a horn, it seems clear that "This sod has bound us" must be a misprint for "This bond has bound us", the reading of the text published in 1951 from a typescript which descends from George Moore and of a carbon typescript in the Berg Collection, New York Public Library. The emendation of "sod" to "bond" has therefore been admitted into the new *Poems*, though in all other respects the text of *A Broad Sheet* has been preferred to that of the posthumous edition.[22]

The remaining poem that requires comment is the third part of "Three Songs to the Same Tune", a work removed from the "Parnell's Funeral and Other Poems" section in the new *Poems* for reasons explained in Chapter IV. Here the version found in *A Broadside* for December 1935 has been preferred to that contained in *A Full Moon by March*, published by Macmillan, London, on 22 November 1935. A crucial passage is ll. 4–5, which Yeats had revised in the earlier printings. *A Full Moon in March* reads

---

[22] See VP1 1200–1. The other songs from the published *Diarmuid and Grania* were not printed in Yeats's lifetime and therefore have not been included in the new *Poems*.

> Troy backed its Helen; Troy died and adored;
> Great nations, blossom above;

while *A Broadside* offers

> Troy backed its Helen, Troy died and adored;
> Great nations blossom above;

A Broadside is thus identical to the proper reading of the same lines as found in second part of "Three Marching Songs". Moreover, on 14 June 1939 Mrs Yeats instructed Thomas Mark to eliminate the comma in "Great nations, blossom above" in "Three Marching Songs" "because it alters the meaning". The manuscripts and typescripts for "Three Marching Songs" confirm the correctness of her assertion.[23]

One emendation, however, has been admitted into the new *Poems*. The comma at the end of l. 19 in *A Broadside* has been changed to a semi-colon, as in ll. 9 and 29 and the version printed in *A Full Moon in March*.

[23] In "W. B. Yeats", *TLS*, 20 April 1946, p. 187, Grattan Freyer argues in favour of the comma in "Great nations, blossom above", but he does not take into account the manuscript evidence.

Conclusion:
Towards the Next Edition

From what we have seen, it should be clear that for Yeats's poems a truly "Definitive Edition" — as the term is understood by most readers — is impossible. The process of editing Yeats's poems is one of gradual improvement, not one of sudden shifts from corrupt to perfect texts. Thus the only proper claim for the new *Poems*, one which I trust the work justifies, is that it is an advance on the previous editions. It will doubtless not be free of misprints; these can always be corrected in a new printing. More importantly, the new *Poems* is only as authoritative as the materials on which it is based. Given the lack of a comprehensive survey and catalogue of Yeats's manuscripts, it is almost certain that I have neglected some relevant documents outside the major collections. Moreover, not all of Yeats's manuscripts are in public collections, and some private collectors are not anxious to have their holdings known, examined, or reproduced.

Two items which I have been unable to locate may have a special significance for the next edition of Yeats's poetry. One is the annotated copy of *The Wanderings of Oisin* which Mrs Yeats gave to Thomas Mark. This must surely still exist. When it becomes available, it will be possible to verify the text of the 1943 edition of *Mosada* and perhaps to make further changes in the early poems not reprinted after *The Wanderings of Oisin*. The second "missing" item is the page proofs for the 1933 *Collected Poems*. Here it is less certain that they survive, although it is difficult to believe that Mark would have allowed them to be destroyed. Should they be discovered, it will be possible to analyse properly the differences between the final proofs for the 1932 Edition de Luxe *Poems* and the *Collected Poems*.

There are, of course, numerous other items which may or may

not exist, such as the typescripts which Mrs Yeats sent to the
London Mercury in October 1938. But no matter how much new
material comes to light, the editing of Yeats's poems will always
remain as much an art as a science, and individual readers will
always be required to evaluate the texts offered them in any particular edition against their own sense of Yeats as a poet.[1] In doing
so they can follow no better advice than that offered by Yeats himself, commenting on Dante Gabriel Rossetti's editing of the poems
of William Blake:

> He also made many corrections of metre and grammar in poems
> which had been printed before, and avowed doing so, and
> against this little can be said, for the originals were in print and
> posterity could judge.[2]

[1] For example, in "Reflections on the Status of the Text", *Cumberland Poetry
Review*, 1, No. 1 (Winter 1981), 64–71, Hugh Kenner has reminded us of
Yeats's revision of the opening line of "Sailing to Byzantium" to "Old men
should quit a country where the young" for the BBC broadcast of "My Own
Poetry" on 3 July 1937, an event recalled most clearly by V. C. Clinton-
Baddeley in "Reading Poetry with W. B. Yeats", *London Magazine*, 4, No. 12
(December 1957), 47–53. When Clinton-Baddeley mentioned that the first line
as printed was difficult to read aloud, Yeats replied that "It's the worst piece of
syntax I ever wrote": "That evening he met me in the lift at Broadcasting
House. In his hand he had a copy of his poems with a new line scrawled in"
(p. 52). Although Kenner mistakenly suggests that "a year or so after the BBC
incident Yeats corrected his texts for the Definitive Edition", he argues that
nevertheless "it is difficult to repress a suspicion that editors and anthologists
would long since have incorporated the revised reading if it struck anyone as a
rhetorical improvement. It seems not to (it certainly does not so strike me), and
we all connive at overruling an auctorial intrusion with which we should feel
stuck had he chanced to hand it to a printer" (p. 66). I would add only that this
particular change strikes me as a "nonce revision", one made for the purposes of
oral presentation but not intended for publication. Had Yeats wanted to retain
the new line, he would have doubtless copied it into one of the corrected copies
of *Collected Poems* cited in Chapter 2. "The copy of his poems" noted by
Clinton-Baddeley has not yet been traced (this might well have been a
typescript of poems prepared for the broadcast rather than an actual volume).
[2] "The Writings of William Blake", *The Bookman*, 4, No. 23 (August 1896),
146.

Appendix A:
Poems by "Y." in *Hibernia*, 1882–83

In "When Was Yeats First Published?" Micheál Ó hAodha has suggested that eleven poems signed with the initial "Y." in the Dublin periodical *Hibernia* from April 1882 to July 1883 might be the work of W. B. Yeats.[1] O hAodha offers two pieces of evidence. First, a copy of the initial volume of the journal in the National Library of Ireland has two inscriptions, assigned by O hAodha to the librarian and scholar Richard Irvine Best. One attributes an unsigned article on Robert Louis Stevenson, "A New Writer of English Prose" (2 January 1882), to T. W. Lyster, a predecessor of Best at the National Library of Ireland. The other inscription is found after the poem "Sweet Aura!" in the issue for July 1882 and reads "? W. B. Yeats". Secondly, O hAodha points to an exchange of correspondence in the *Irish Book Lover*. In the April–May 1919 number, "T.C.D." had asked for information about *Hibernia*. The reply, presumably from the editor of the *Irish Book Lover*, John S. Crone, gives a description of the journal and states that the contributors included "W. B. Yeats over his initial 'Y.'"[2] Moreover, the following issue of the *Irish Book Lover* contains a lengthy and detailed account of *Hibernia* from someone who signs himself "An Old Contributor." Displaying an intimate knowledge of the workings of *Hibernia*, he adds to the list of contributors, stating that his names are "in addition to those mentioned" in the earlier number of the *Irish Book Lover*.[3] By implication, then,

---

[1] Micheál Ó hAodha, "When Was Yeats First Published?", *Irish Times*, 5 June 1965, p. 10. The article was reprinted, without the text of "Sonnet", in *Éire-Ireland*, 2, No. 2 (Summer 1967), 67–71. It might be noted that *Hibernia* was published only from January 1882 to July 1883 and has no connection with the current periodical of the same name.

[2] *Irish Book Lover*, 10, Nos. 9–10 (April–May 1919), 93.

[3] *Irish Book Lover*, 10, Nos. 11–12 (June–July 1919), 110–11.

"An Old Contributor" would seem to confirm that Yeats's work appeared in *Hibernia*.

The evidence against Yeats's authorship, on the other hand, seems formidable. Although Hone states that "at seventeen he [Yeats] began to write verses",[4] it is clear that Yeats's father discouraged publication at such an early age. Writing to Edward Dowden on 7 January 1884, six months after the final poem by "Y." in *Hibernia*, John Butler Yeats remarks that "Of course I never dreamed of publishing the effort of a youth of eighteen".[5] Secondly, most of the poems in *Hibernia* have an indication that they were written in either "Surrey" or "London", neither of which Yeats is known to have visited at the appropriate time. Thirdly, so far as I know there is no manuscript material for the poems in Yeats's papers in the collection of Michael B. Yeats or elsewhere, whereas manuscripts do survive for the very early poetic dramas of ca. 1883 and later. Finally, it seems to me quite unlikely that the correspondence in the *Irish Book Lover* would have escaped the notice of Allan Wade, who had published his first bibliography of Yeats's writings in 1908 and who was continually adding to it and revising it. Yet Wade makes no mention in either his *Bibliography* or the *Letters* of the poems in *Hibernia*. Indeed, I think it is conceivable that he saw the statements in the *Irish Book Lover*, wrote or asked Yeats about the question, and received a negative answer.

It is, of course, also possible to argue against Yeats's authorship of the poems on the basis of their content, themes, and style. To me, at least, such a discussion would but make *more* remote the possibility that "Y." is in fact Yeats. However, since such arguments must always be subjective, and since the only file of *Hibernia* appears to be the one in the National Library of Ireland, I have decided to reproduce the eleven poems, allowing individual readers to weigh the existing evidence and conjecture and to reach their own conclusions.

[4] Joseph Hone, *W. B. Yeats, 1865–1939*, 2nd ed. (London: Macmillan, 1962), p. 34. In his edition of *J. B. Yeats: Letters to His Son W. B. Yeats and Others, 1869–1922* (New York: E. P. Dutton, 1946), p. 52, n. 1, Hone states that "W. B. Yeats wrote his first poems in 1882, just before he was seventeen".

[5] *J. B. Yeats: Letters to His Son W. B. Yeats and Others, 1869–1922*, p. 52.

SONNET.

I saw a shepherd youth, with fixëd gaze,
  As one dream-haunted in his waking hours,
  Hold listlessly a coronal of flowers,
The while his sheep, in unaccustomed ways,
Looked meekly back for guidance. Yet he lay,
  While the still shade like a sweet mystery
  Enveloped him, as though he could not see:
Nor heard: but evermore a[l]thro' the day
With little pauses (like the Nightingale's)
  Of charmëd silence, on his lips awoke
  The same soft simple notes that scarcely broke
To sound, and called no echo from the vales.
Dear heart! their echo in myself I find:
Turning the same love-thought for ever in my mind.

[*Hibernia*, 1, No. 4 (1 April 1882), 55]   Y.

"THE WINGS OF A DOVE."

Some with the wings of song can reach
  The clear, calm, and eternal heights:
Some with the music of their speech
  Fill life with varying delights:
Some from communing with the skies,
  Catch heavenly glimpses; from the stone
Some bid imprisoned Ariel rise;
  Ah, me!—O love: and love alone!

Yet love can change—from love I know,—
  The dullest heart into a shrine:
Our love is weak till our lives grow
  True symbols of Life Divine.
Love blindeth? Nay, he clears our eyes
  To look beyond earth's narrow zone;—
Then break they bonds, my soul! and rise
  Upon the wings of love alone!

[*Hibernia*, 1, No. 5 (1 May 1882), 75]   Y.

LOVE'S SILENCES.

Buzzings haunt the honied shadows
  Of the chestnut's broadening tent;
Hear the kine low in the meadows
  With a measureless content:

Sparrows quarrel, chat, and glitter,
    Like quick children, as they dip:
'Neath our eaves the swallows twitter,
    As with human fellowship:
Nature is awake and singing:
Poet Love, what song to that full chorus art thou bringing?
    Dove-like, tell thy fluty numbers
      One sweet word that never tires?
    Lark-like, bring'st our sunny slumbers
      Echoes from angelic lyres?
    Every change from grief to pleasure
      Dost in one great hymn combine—
    In one yearning passionate measure,
      Hallowed by thy lips divine? . . .
    Nay, Love, nay,—thou art not singing:
Only such as serve thee know the thoughts within thee springing!
[*Hibernia*, 1, No. 6 (June 1882), 92]   Y.

"SWEET AURA!"

With the homely shepherds in fellowship,
    Under the feathery elms I drowse;
Like the tears of a lover, the sere leaves drip
    From the kindling green of the arching boughs.

The rose to-day is consumed with desire;
    The dry air pulses; the fierce heat beats
To the heart of the forest in shafts of fire;
    In the thin wan grass how the faint flock bleats!

As the sheep stray, panting, the distant tide
    With a gleam invites; with the lambs we go;
On the lake's smooth bosom the calm swans glide,
    Floating like delicate flakes of snow.

We have left the sheltering woods, in the blaze
    Of untempered noon, for the open glade;
And we still may see, through a pearly haze,
    A Danaë shower in the night-black shade.

Laid 'neath the close-knit hawthorn leaves
    On a bank, the flock is folded to rest;
But list,—a rustle! the light wave heaves!
    God bless thee, kindly breeze from the West!
Surrey.   Y.
[*Hibernia*, 1, No. 8 (July 1882), 106]

SONNET.

I sang of thee, when Autumn's hectic glow
    Forecast the dissolution of the Year:
I sang of thee, when Winter laid him low,
    O'erstrewing his white pall with roses sere;
And when his Heir, laughing away a tear,
    New life infused into our sluggish blood,
My strains rang out amid Spring's carols clear,
    And my thoughts burgeoned in each leaf and bud.
And now that Summer, more mature and ripe,
    Flushes with grace the work by Spring begun,
I follow Pan with imitative pipe,
    Warbling thy praises 'neath a quickening sun:
Nor think a floral crown to-day to win,
    But wait my share, when Love his harvest gathers in.
(Surrey.)   Y.
[*Hibernia*, 1, No. 8 (August 1882), 123)

GOING!

The clock's quick tick—the bell's slow boom,
    The bright street's rattling riot,—
The shifting shadows in my room—
    The broadening lull and quiet—
The ebb of life that flowed around—
    Fresh evening breezes blowing,—
Some near, but late unnoted sound—
    All tell me time is going:
And yet thou comest not, my heart,
    Altho' the time is going!

So have I seen with vapours dun
    The grinding City sheeted,
So watched the purpled sickly sun
    By hissing showers defeated;
So felt the arrows of the East
    Slay Spring's first greenness growing—
And now from her unfinished feast
    Reluctant Summer's going,—
And yet thou comest not, my heart,
    Tho' Summer kind is going!

Love o'er my cares cast flower on flower
    As on with time he hasted;

His sweet thoughts tranced me many an hour:
  Thank God it was not wasted!
You filled my dreams alone, my sweet,—
  You set hope's sunshine glowing,
Then bid me wait your ventruous feet—
  Still time alas! is going:
. . . And I must follow my hot heart
  That straight to thine is going!

[*Hibernia*, 1, No. 9 (September 1882), 144]   Y.

SONNET.

How am I pained that Love, the urchin wild,
  Putting his own keen arrows to the test,
Hath pierced his side! And yet he wanly smiled
  To see them purpled with his ichor blest.
I gathered him, deep-breathing, voiceless, mild,
  To the protecting cradle of my breast,
And, as a mother her unquiet child,
  Lulled him with tender lullabies to rest.

I gave him poppy and mandragora,
  But feared lest he might sleep to wake no more;
  I bound his wound,—anointing the fell dart;
Still his large sleepless eyes transfixed with awe:
  Fevering, the rosy salve aside he tore. . .
    Yet lives! but ever clasps the Arrow to his heart.
London.   Y.

[*Hibernia*, 1, No. 10 (October 1882), 159]

L'ENVOI.

Here must I bid adieu, my sweet;
  But will you take these simple songs
Whose rhythm my very pulses beat,
  Whose only worth to Love belongs?

How cold they read!—yet, ere you close,
  If 'neath the tropes and rhymes you look,
You'll find my heart, like a crushed rose,
  Between the pages of the book!
London.   Y.

[*Hibernia*, 1, No. 12 (December 1882), 188]

RECALL.

Daily, hourly, as I think of you,
  Though at first that dear fond face I see
  Only, smiling back my dreams to me,
Like Love's star in yon unfading blue,
Yet a little while, and every scene
  That hath known you, circles you again,
  And I live my second life as then;
Owning all of love that once hath been.
And, even as the flutter of green leaves,
  Flash of summer lightnings, and wild rains,
    Gladdening gusts from one tumultous shore,
Come again: so Memory ever weaves
  Into lasting hues my joys and pains,
    For that embodied Hope whom He shall yet restore!
Surrey.   Y.

[*Hibernia*, 2, No. 4 (May 1883), 71]

SONNET.

Here am I lost in verdurous solitudes
  Which ne'er the city's murmurs hoarse invade,
Where as a dove calm Contemplation broods,
  And even my dreams are sunshine flecked with shade.
  The answering of the birds adown the glade
Echoes like faint, low laughter; the plumed grass
  Trembles, and breathings sweet the boughs pervade,
As though the spirits of the woodland pass.
O my Egeria! oft to such a spot
From books and men has thy dear image brought
  Thy love, to pour into his heart thy lore—
To ban whate'er thine innocence might wrong,
To show the living stream that makes men strong,
  And bid him drink, and know his cares no more!
Surrey.   Y.

[*Hibernia*, 2, No. 5 (June 1883), 79]

LOVE'S CLAIRVOYANCE.

I think I hear you trilling some old song
  Burdened with sobs and laughter—and again
  Be mute, as with a sudden throb of pain:

Till the white keys your fingers steal along,
Releasing your sad thoughts in a clear flood
  Of music weird and strange. Or else you take
Some book that casts you in a tender mood,
  In which you dream and dream, nor would awake.
I see you breathing life into the stark
    Cold canvas—then cast down the brush, and pass
    Amid the languid flowers and humid grass,
And with rapt simple soul outsoar the lark;—
But whether linked with earth, or heavenward caught,
My star forever moves in the orbit of your thought.
London.   Y.

[*Hibernia*, 2, No. 6 (July 1883), 98]

Appendix B: Some Sources for the Poems in Yeats's Plays

A. "Two Songs Rewritten for the Tune's Sake", I ["My Paistin Finn is my sole desire"]

Based on a well-known Irish song, *Paistín Fionn*. Among the translations available to Yeats were those by John D'Alton in James Hardiman's *Irish Minstrelsy* (1831), Edward Walsh (*Irish Popular Songs*, 1847) and Samuel Ferguson (*Lays of the Western Gael*, 1874). Yeats's version is closest to that by Ferguson. Given below is the text from *Irish Minstrelsy*, ed. H. Halliday Sparling [2nd ed.] (London: Walter Scott, 1888), pp. 292–3, with the refrain printed only after the first stanza since it does not change thereafter.

O my fair Pastheen is my heart's delight;
Her gay heart laughs in her blue eyes bright;
Like the apple blossom her bosom white,
And her neck like the swan's on a March morn bright!
    Then, Oro, come with me! come with me! come with me!
    Oro, come with me! brown girl, sweet!
    And O I would go through snow and sleet
    If you would come with me, brown girl, sweet!

Love of my heart, my fair Pastheen!
Her cheeks are as red as the rose's sheen,
But my lips have tasted no more, I ween,
Than the glass I drank to the health of my queen!

Were I in the town, where's mirth and glee,
Or 'twixt two barrels of barley bree,
With my fair Pastheen upon my knee,
'Tis I would drink to her pleasantly!

129

Nine night I lay in longing and pain,
Betwixt two bushes, beneath the rain,
Thinking to see you, love, once again;
But whistle and call were in vain!

I'll leave my people, both friend and foe;
From all the girls in the world I'll go;
But from you, sweetheart, O never! O no!
Till I lie in the coffin, stretched, cold and low!

B. ["I will go cry with the woman"]

In *The United Irishman* for 5 May 1902, Yeats indicated that the
song was "suggested to me by some old Gaelic folk-song" (VP1
234). The probable source is Lady Gregory, who published a version of "Faired-haired Donough" in an article on "West Irish Folk
Ballads" in *The Monthly Review* for October 1902. A revised version of the essay became the chapter on "West Irish Ballads" in her
Poets and Dreamers (London: John Murray, 1903), the source
(p. 49) of the text given below.

"It was bound fast here you saw him, and you wondered to see
        him,
   Our fair-haired Donough, and he after being condemned;
   There was a little white cap on him in place of a hat,
   And a hempen rope in the place of a neckcloth.

"I am after walking here all through the night,
   Like a young lamb in a great flock of sheep;
   My breast open, my hair loosened out,
   And how did I find my brother but stretched before me!

"The first place I cried my fill was at the top of the lake;
   The second place was at the foot of the gallows;
   The third place was at the head of your dead body
   Among the Gall, and my own head as if cut in two.

"If you were with me in the place you had a right to be,
   Down in Sligo or down in Ballinrobe,
   It is the gallows would be broken, it is the rope would be cut,
   And fair-haired Donough going home by the path.

"O fair-haired Donough, it is not the gallows was fit for you;
But to be going to the barn, to be threshing out the straw;
To be turning the plough to the right hand and to the left,
To be putting the red side of the soil uppermost.

"O fair-haired Donough, O dear brother,
It is well I know who it was took you away from me;
Drinking from the cup, putting a light to the pipe,
And walking in the dew in the cover of the night.

"O Michael Malley, O scourge of misfortune!
My brother was no calf of a vagabond cow;
But a well-shaped boy on a height or a hillside,
To knock a low pleasant sound out of a hurling-stick.

"And fair-haired Donough, is not that the pity,
You that would carry well a spur or a boot;
I would put clothes in the fashion on you from cloth that
    would be lasting;
I would send you out like a gentleman's son.

"O Michael Malley, may your sons never be in one another's
    company;
May your daughters never ask a marriage portion of you;
The two ends of the table are empty, the house is filled.
And fair-haired Donough, my brother, is stretched out.

"There is a marriage portion coming home from Donough,
But it is not cattle nor sheep nor horses;
But tobacco and pipes and white candles,
And it will not be begrudged to them that will use it."

C. ["The spouse of Naoise, Erin's woe"]

The poem is based on the second stanza of "Eire's Maid Is She" by
William O'Heffernan the Blind. Yeats could have read the work
in several sources, including Edward Walsh's *Reliques of Irish
Jacobite Poetry*, 2nd ed. (Dublin: John O'Daly, 1866), pp. 78–81,
the source of the text given below:

> In Druid vale alone I lay,
> Oppress'd with care, to weep the day;
> My death I owed one sylph-like she,
> Of witchery rare, *Beith Eirionn Í*

The spouse of Naisi, Erin's wo,
The dame that laid proud Illium low,
Their charms would fade, their fame would flee,
Match'd with my fair, *Beih Eirionn I!*

Behold her tresses unconfin'd,
In wanton ringlets woo the wind,
Or sweep the sparkling dew-drops free,
My heart's dear maid, *Beih Eirionn I!*

Fierce passion's slave, from hope exil'd,
Weak, wounded, weary, woful, wild;
Some magic spell she wove for me,
That peerless maid, *Beih Eirionn I!*

But O! one noon I clomb a hill,
To sigh alone—to weep my fill,
And there Heaven's mercy brought to me
My treasure rare, *Beih Eirionn I!*

D. ["There's broth in the pot for you, old man"]

In 1904 Yeats claimed that "The words and the air of 'There's Broth in the Pot' were taken down from an old woman known as Cracked Mary, who wanders about the plains of Aidhne, and who sometimes sees unearthly riders on white horses coming through stony fields to her hovel in the night time" (VP1 254). Evidently, Cracked Mary must have been familiar with *Ancient and Modern Scottish Songs, Heroic Ballads, Etc.* (Edinburgh: printed by John Wotherspoon for James Dickson and Charles Elliot, 1776), which includes "I wish that you were dead, Goodman" (II, 207–8). A typed copy of the poem from the second edition (also 1776) is preserved in the collection of Michael B. Yeats (who, incidentally, has identified the air as "a folk tune called 'Jack the Journeyman'"). The text below is taken from the first edition of *Ancient and Modern Scottish Songs*:

> *I wish that you were dead, Goodman,*
> *   And a green sod on your head, goodman,*
> *   That I might ware my widowhood,*
> *   Upon a ranting highlandman.*

There's sax eggs in the pan, goodman,
There's sax eggs in the pan, goodman,
There's ane to you, and twa to me,
And three to our JOHN HIGHLANDMAN,
  I wish, &c.

There's beef into the pat, goodman,
There's beef into the pat, goodman,
The banes for you, and the brew for me,
And the beef for our JOHN HIGHLANDMAN.
  I wish, &c.

There's sax horse in the stable, goodman,
There's sax horse in the stable, goodman,
There's ane to you, and twa to me,
And three to our JOHN HIGHLANDMAN.
  I wish, &c.

There's sax ky in the byre, goodman,
There's sax ky in the byre, goodman,
There's nane o' them yours, but there's twa of them mine,
And the lave is our JOHN HIGHLANDMAN'S.
  I wish, &c.

E. ["O come all ye airy bachelors"]

The beginning of this song is the first line of "The Airy Bachelor",
which Yeats could have read in the *Journal of the Irish Folk Song
Society*, 2, Nos. 1–2 (1905), 33: "Come all you airy bachelors, a
warning take by me". The remainder seems based on a ballad
usually called "Van Diemen's Land" or "The Gallant Poachers".
Yeats could have read it under the latter title in the *Journal of the
Folk-Song Society*, 1, No. 4 (1902), 142–3:

Come all you gallant poachers, that ramble free from care,
  That walk out of a moon-light night with your dog, your gun,
      and snare;
  Where the lofty hare and pheasant you have at your command,
  Not thinking that your last career is on Van Diemen's Land.

There was poor Tom Brown from Nottingham, Jack Williams,
    and poor Joe
Were three as daring poachers as the country well does know;
At night they were trapannèd by the keeper's hideous hand,
And for fourteen years transported were unto Van Diemen's
    Land.

Oh! when we sailed from England we landed at the bay,
We had rotten straw for bedding, we dared not to say nay;
Our cots were fenced with fire, we slumber where we can,
To drive away the wolves and tigers upon Van Diemen's Land.

Oh! when that we were landed, upon that fatal shore,
The planters they came flocking round full twenty score or
    more;
They ranked us up like horses, and sold us out of hand,
They yoked us to the plough, my boys, to plough Van Diemen's
    Land.

There was one girl from England, Susan Summers was her
    name,
For fourteen years transported was, we all well knew the same;
Our planter bought her freedom, and he married her out of
    hand,
Good usage then she gave to us, upon Van Diemen's Land.

Often, when I am slumbering, I have a pleasant dream,
With my sweet girl I am sitting, down by some purling stream,
Through England I am roaming, with her at my command,
Then waken, broken-hearted, upon Van Diemen's Land.

God bless our wives and families, likewise that happy shore,
That isle of sweet contentment, which we shall see no more;
As for our wretched females, see them we seldom can,
There are twenty to one woman upon Van Diemen's Land.

Come, all you gallant poachers, give ear unto my song,
It is a bit of good advice, although it is not long:
Lay by your dog and snare; to you I do speak plain,
If you knew the hardship we endure you ne'er would poach
    again.

F. ["O, Johnny Gibbons, my five hundred healths to you!"]

The two couplets from *The Unicorn from the Stars*, printed together in the new *Poems*, are based on the fourth stanza of "The Whiteboys", sometimes ascribed to Raftery. Yeats would have come across the poem in Douglas Hyde's *Songs Ascribed to Raftery* (Dublin: Gill and Son, 1903), p. 197:

O Johnny Gibbons, my five hundred farewells to you,
    You are long from me away in Germany;
It was your heart, without deceitfulness, that was ever (given)
    to joyousness,
And now on this hill, above, we are weak of help.
It is told us from the mouth of the author
    That the sloop whose crew was not baptised shall fire at us,
And unless you come for a relief to us in the times of hardship,
    We are a great pity, beneath the tops of valleys.

G. ["O, the lion shall lose his strength"]

The song is based on an Irish poem translated by Lady Gregory in *Poets and Dreamers* (p. 89) as follows:

When the lion shall lose its strength,
    And the bracket Thistle begin to pine,
The Harp shall sound sweet, sweet at length,
    Between the eight and the nine.

The versions used in the early editions of *The Unicorn from the Stars* are quite close to Lady Gregory's rendering. Yeats revised the song for the 1934 *Collected Plays*.

Douglas Hyde also provides two different versions of the poem, in *Songs Ascribed to Raftery* (p. 271) and *The Religious Songs of Connacht* (Dublin: M. H. Gill & Son; London: T. Fisher Unwin, 1906), I, 261, describing it as an "old prophecy".

H. ["Three that are watching my time to run"]

The poem is based on the opening stanza of "The Worms, the Children, and the Devil" from Douglas Hyde's *Religious Songs of*

Connacht, I, 51. Hyde offers two versions of the stanza, with the first being closer to that in *The Unicorn from the Stars*:

> Three there be, watching for my death,
> Although they are ever with me (?)
> Alas that they be not hanged with a gad,
> The Devil, the children, and the worm.
>
> . . . .
>
> There be three—my heart it saith—
> Wish the death of me infirm,
> Would that they were hanged on a tree,
> All three, Children, Devil, Worm.

I. ["I was going the road one day"]

Yeats explains that he "put into English rhyme three of the many verses of a Gaelic ballad" (VP 778) for use in *The Hour-Glass*. His source was a translation by Lady Gregory of an Irish folksong, published as "The Noble Enchanter" in the 1901 Christmas number of *The Irish Homestead*:

> I was going the road one fine day,
> O, the brown and the yellow ale!
> And I met with a man that was no right man,
> O, love of my heart.

He asked was the young woman with me my daughter, and I said she was my married wife.

He asked would I lend her for an hour or a day. "Oh, I would not do that, but I would like to do what is fair. Let you take the upper path and I will go by the road, and whoever she will follow, let him belong to her forever."

He took the upper path and I took the road, and she followed after him, he being in his youth.

She stayed walking there the length of three quarters, and she came home after, Mary without shame.

She asked me how was I in my health. "As is good with my friends and bad with my enemies. And what would you do if I would die from you?" "I would put a coffin of yellow gold on you."

When myself heard those fine words, I lay down and died there. And there were two that went to the woods for timber, and they brought back a half board of holly and a half board of alder.

They put me into the boarded coffin, and four yards of the ugliest sack about me, and they lifted me up on their shoulders. "Throw him now into the best hole in the street."

"Oh, wait, wait, lay me down, till I tell you a little story about women; a little story today and a little story tomorrow, and a little story every day of the quarter."

> And but that my own little mother was a woman,
>   O, the brown and the yellow ale!
> I would tell you another little story about women,
>   O, love of my heart!

The following three passages have not been admitted into the new *Poems*.

1. ["Philomel, I've listened oft"] [VP1 247]
Except for the change of "nigh" to "near", the two lines which appear in *The Pot of Broth* are a verbatim quotation from Edward Lysaght's "Kate of Garnavilla" (the first two lines of the second stanza). A convenient source for Yeats would have been *The Irish Song Book*, ed. Alfred Perceval Graves (London: T. Fisher Unwin, 1894), p. 22.

2. ["'Twas at the dance at Dermody's that first I caught a sight of her"] [VP1 247]
Except for the change of "Darmody's" to "Dermody's", this line in *The Pot of Broth* is a verbatim quotation from Francis A. Fahy's "Little Mary Cassidy" (the first line of the second stanza), which Yeats also might have found in Graves's *Irish Song Book*, p. 115.

3. ["When you were an acorn on the tree-top"] [VP1 519]
This four-line poem from *On Baile's Strand* was published by Yeats as "A Folk Verse" in the "Anonymous" section of *A Book of Irish Verse* (London: Methuen, 1895), p. 249. Yeats added the hyphen in "tree-top" for the 1907 printing of the play; he added those in "eagle-cock" on the proofs for the 1934 *Collected Plays*.

It is likely that Yeats was given the poem by Douglas Hyde, who includes it in *A Literary History of Ireland* (New York: Charles Scribner's Sons, 1899), p. 541.

Index